LITTLE BOOK OF
CONSPIRACY
Theories

Liam McCann

LITTLE BOOK OF
CONSPIRACY
Theories

First published in the UK in 2014

© Demand Media Limited 2014

www.demand-media.co.uk

Printed and bound in Europe

ISBN 978-1-910270-19-6

Contents

Introduction

We live in an era when every natural disaster, unnatural death and momentous event is brought into our homes by television and the internet within minutes of it happening. But we've grown weary of being force-fed news by people we no longer trust so it's little wonder that the most dramatic events of our time become shrouded in mystery. We like to question official reports and believe that other forces may be at work, although we hope that the mysteries surrounding the events are eventually solved.

The recent disappearance of the Malaysian Airlines Boeing 777 in March 2014 is a classic case in point: the media breaks what would normally be a tragic but routine event – a plane crash – but then we learn the aircraft is missing rather than down, off course and not responding, and probably flew thousands of miles before disappearing from radar. The event then snowballs into a media sensation with everyone from the qualified to the conspiracy theorist offering their opinion. Several weeks later, we are bombarded with possible explanations from the likely – pilot error or catastrophic system failure – to the outrageous – abducted by aliens, and we are unsure what to believe. As the mystery deepens, we find ourselves trawling the internet and news channels for explanations and, when we find an official report unconvincing, we offer our own theories instead. At the time of writing the aircraft is still missing but presumed crashed in the Southern

Indian Ocean, most likely after an attempted hijacking.

A similar situation arose in the wake of the loss of KAL-007 off Sakhalin Island in September 1983. Despite an extensive search for the missing 747 its wreckage wasn't discovered for a month, during which time conspiracy theories and accusations abounded. The explanation for the disappearance was complex but the truth, when it finally surfaced, only confirmed the fact that most mysteries can be solved by piecing together a critical chain of events and mistakes are almost always made during investigations.

The Korean Airlines jet strayed off course after the pilots forgot to activate the inertial navigation system. It crossed Soviet territory, was confused with an American spy plane and was shot down by a pilot who should have taken

Korean Airlines Flight 007, 1 September 1983

ABOVE The crew of KAL-007 forgot to set the aircraft's inertial navigation system and it veered north of its planned route into Soviet airspace

over subjects and people as diverse as AIDS, Pearl Harbour, William Shakespeare, Paul McCartney (who was supposed to be dead at the height of Beatlemania), the *Titanic*, Marilyn Monroe's death, Robert Kennedy's assassination, green power and a new world order. With AIDS the theory goes that HIV was a man-made virus designed to halt the human population explosion, but surely not even the most irresponsible scientist would unleash such a potent killer.

There are rumours that Winston Churchill was so desperate for the United States to enter the Second World War – Britain was only a few months from being forced into submission by the U-boats sinking the convoys carrying vital supplies – that he ordered plans, ship positions and the defences surrounding Pearl Harbour to be leaked to the Japanese. Churchill had previous in regard to condemning Allied servicemen to death when he sank the French fleet in North Africa rather than letting it fall into German hands so there could be some truth to this hypothesis.

the time to identify it as a passenger aircraft. A simple but tragic explanation for an event at the height of the Cold War when mutual distrust between the superpowers was such that any unusual incident spawned theories and triggered accusations.

Conspiracy theories have erupted

Edward Vere'' Earle of Oxford
Lord high Chamberlaine of Eng.^{ld}
Married 1.st Ann Daughter to
Wm Cecil Lord Burghley 2.nd
Eliz Daughter to Thos Trentham
of Roucester in Com: Stafford
and died 24.th of June 1604

1575

When the evidence is analysed in greater detail, however, the attack can be attributed solely to the Japanese.

The popular conspiracy theory concerning William Shakespeare contends that he didn't actually write any plays, and there is some circumstantial evidence to support this: there are references in the works to several events in Edward de Vere's life and codes in

ABOVE Edward de Vere is thought by some to have penned the works attributed to Shakespeare

the writing supposedly out him as the author. The 17th Earl of Oxford was a renowned poet and the theory gained momentum after the film *Anonymous* used the theory as its premise. Playwright Christopher Marlowe is another contender to have authored the works. He was about to be imprisoned for atheism so the rumour goes that he faked his own death and continued writing under the Shakespeare name to protect the truth. William Stanley, 6th Earl of Derby, also has a claim as he ran a popular theatre company, signed his works Will and supposedly based Polonius on William Cecil, to whom he was related by marriage. As Shakespeare came from humble beginnings and relative obscurity, theorists claim that an educated aristocrat like those mentioned, or even Sir Francis Bacon – who had knowledge of royal courts and access to the establishment – must have written the works instead. However, no direct evidence supports the theories and Shakespeare's reputation was never questioned during his lifetime or for two centuries afterwards. Indeed his contemporaries – actors and playwrights alike – were unanimous in their praise for Shakespeare as an author and a

person. And it is his factual mistakes and inconsistencies that mark him out as a grammar school pupil rather than a university-educated aristocrat, something that would be almost impossible to fake.

In what would have been an outrageous deception, the *Titanic* and

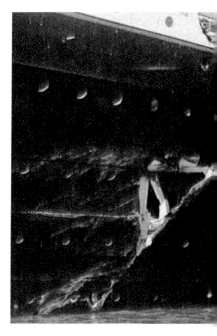

her sister *Olympic* were apparently swapped before the former's maiden voyage in a clandestine insurance scam. The White Star Line was losing money and the Olympic had been badly damaged in a collision with the cruiser HMS *Hawke*, so the line decided to swap the ships overnight in Belfast and deliberately sink the *Olympic*. Unfortunately, the rescue ships that were supposed to be on hand to pick up survivors were late arriving and the plan failed spectacularly and tragically. However, although very few identifying marks were found on the wreck, the interior and exterior layouts of the ships

LEFT Damage to the RMS Olympic caused by the collision with HMS Hawke

were slightly different and it is the *Titanic* that lies in a watery grave more than two miles down.

The death of Marilyn Monroe has been variously attributed to the Kennedys – she was having affairs with both Robert and John and they were afraid she was going to embarrass the family – suicide, and an accidental overdose. When all the evidence is examined, conspiracy theorists will probably have to accept that the latter is the most likely. All of the autopsy findings regarding stomach contents and the timing of ingestion can be explained rationally and there's no reason to suspect third-party involvement.

Robert Kennedy's assassination was witnessed by scores of people in close proximity but some mysteries do remain. Why, for example, did coroner Thomas Noguchi insist that the fatal headshot had been fired from a range of no more than an inch or two when no one in the kitchen of the Ambassador Hotel believed 24 year-old Palestinian

immigrant Sirhan Sirhan had got closer than several feet? And why does the acoustic evidence appear to show more than eight shots being fired, impossible if the weapon used by Sirhan was the only gun discharged in the room?

The proximity of the headshot *can* be explained by eyewitness testimony, however. As Sirhan approached, Kennedy turned to his left to shake

LEFT Could the ships have been switched?

ABOVE Marilyn Monroe almost certainly died in bed of an accidental overdose

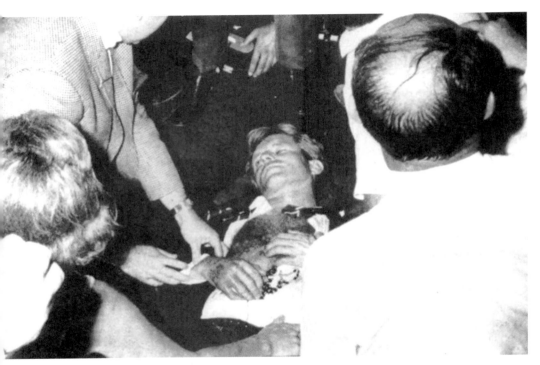

hands with hotel employees and Sirhan could have fired at close range in the confusion. Stanislaw Pruszynski's audiotape doesn't appear to capture the gunshots but acoustic experts have examined it in great detail. Some believe up to 13 shots can be identified, although the majority of analysts agree with the official report that only the eight shots in Sirhan's revolver were fired. Sirhan himself left written evidence that he was going to make an attempt on Kennedy's life, and he confessed to the crime (which his defence team advised him to retract so they could plead diminished responsibility), so the theories don't hold up under scrutiny.

We're tempted to believe that if the oil companies invested in green power, we'd be driving cheap solar-powered cars in no time, but then no one would be buying their oil. There is probably a grain of truth to this. Thirty years ago we were told that fossil fuels would run out early in the 21st century but more reserves are discovered every year. The next fuel boom will be fracking for the vast shale gas reserves that exist in the bedrock so it's doubtful that expensive research into future technologies such as hydrogen fuel cells will take priority over this cheap new power source. Of course the oil company debate is directly linked to the discussion over a new world order as the most powerful people on the planet must be involved in both. But NWO theories are as old as time and it's difficult to believe that mysterious societies or sects are actually controlling our destinies. There is plenty of mystery surrounding the world leaders, power company CEOs and newspaper magnates we see on

ABOVE Mugshot taken of Sirhan Sirhan following his arrest

television every day anyway.

Detailed analysis of the theories mentioned here would fill several books so I've picked five of the most prominent cases to examine.

JFK

The assassination of John F Kennedy was one of the defining moments of the 1960s, and one of the most shocking events of modern times. The young president was popular, rich and had already taken on the Russians over the division of Berlin and during the Cuban Missile Crisis; he had also challenged his country to land a man on the Moon; and he had brought civil rights and the issues surrounding racial segregation to the forefront of domestic politics. But he had also overseen the botched landing at the Bay of Pigs in Cuba, angered the mob by clamping down on organised crime, and upset many within his own party by causing a rift with Vice-President Lyndon Johnson.

Kennedy was born in Brookline,

Massachusetts, in 1917. The family was of Irish descent and moved to the Bronx when he was 10. He joined older brother Joe at school but lived in his shadow and developed a rebellious streak. He also suffered serious health problems as a child – scarlet fever, colitis, Addison's disease, chronic back pain and poor thyroid function – that would dog him his entire life.

Kennedy travelled round Europe during his university years and enlisted in the navy two years after the outbreak of the Second World War. He was

LEFT John F. Kennedy, White House photo portrait, 1961

ABOVE The Kennedy Family at Hyannisport, with John at the rear left

decorated for saving the lives of the crew of his patrol boat so his father encouraged him to run for congress after the war. He then won a seat in the senate in 1952 and married Jacqueline the following year.

At the Democratic National Convention in 1956 he was nominated for vice-president but he finished second, a vote that pleased his father, Joseph, because he didn't believe John's Catholicism or the strength of the Eisenhower camp would have given him much exposure. Four years later, Joe knew the time was right to campaign for the presidency. John overcame opposition from Lyndon Johnson and Adlai Stevenson, and, by July, had secured his party's nomination. He eventually defeated Richard Nixon in one of the closest presidential elections in history.

Kennedy was sworn in at the end of January 1961 and he ended the inauguration with his famous rallying cry: "Ask not what your country can do for you, ask what you can do for your country." He also begged the world to unite against their common enemies:tyranny, poverty, disease and war.

The first weeks of his presidency were spent dismantling the Eisenhower regime. Kennedy was happy to take difficult decisions on racial segregation and human rights, he was successful in turning the recession into a period of growth, and he also lobbied to have the death penalty abolished. His foreign policy would be dominated by the Cold War because Cuba gave the Russians a foothold in the West. There was also growing opposition to the Vietnam War, and he believed his country was being eroded from within by organised crime and its poor record on civil rights.

He was determined to tackle these issues head on but then everything changed on one fateful day in Dallas.

There are many theories over who was responsible for gunning down the 35th American president, but the proponents tend to agree on most of the facts leading up to the shooting on November 22nd 1963.

The trip to Dallas was announced in September, but the itinerary and route the presidential motorcade would take weren't divulged until mid-November. Fearful of the public's reaction to Kennedy because of his unpopularity in Texas, he was advised not to make the trip, but the president would not be deterred and the police undertook the

ABOVE Dealey Plaza

there were no problems reported on the route. At 12.29pm, the motorcade turned right onto Houston Street before slowing to around 10 miles an hour and turning sharp left onto Elm Street beneath the Texas School Book Depository in Dealey Plaza. A few moments later, shots echoed around the plaza. Kennedy was struck in his upper back and in the head, and Connally was struck in the back.

The motorcade immediately accelerated under the triple underpass at the western end of the plaza and raced towards Parkland Memorial Hospital. When they arrived at the hospital, two priests were called to administer the last rites and Kennedy was pronounced dead at one o'clock. Connally survived with serious injuries. State law required that Kennedy's autopsy be performed at Parkland Hospital but the Secret Service had already acquired a coffin and told doctors they were taking the body back to Washington.

Back in Dealey Plaza, the police had already searched the book depository and found three spent shell casings by the sixth floor window. Deputy Eugene Boone had also recovered a rifle from the northwest corner of the building on

biggest security operation in the city's history.

The motorcade left Air Force One at Love Field for the journey through downtown Dallas to the Trade Mart building at around 11.40am. It stopped twice so that Kennedy could shake hands with well-wishers before turning right onto Main Street.

The streets in the city centre were packed with people hoping to catch a glimpse of Kennedy with Jackie and

the same floor.

Who fired at the president and why has divided opinion and a nation ever since? The flames of a conspiracy were fuelled by the fact that there were several candidates with the means, motive and opportunity to carry out the assassination.

LEE HARVEY OSWALD

Oswald was born in New Orleans in 1939, but the family moved to Dallas when he was five. He went to school in the local area but was described by teachers and classmates as withdrawn and temperamental. His spelling and writing were extremely poor, possibly due to dyslexia.

In 1952 the family moved to New York but Oswald had more problems at school and a psychological evaluation at a juvenile reformatory suggested he created a vivid fantasy life to compensate for his intellectual and physical inadequacy.

Oswald eventually dropped out and joined the marines to train in radar operations. In 1957 he was cleared to work with confidential files as no worrying background information on him had surfaced, this despite him being overtly pro-Castro and alienating colleagues with his extreme views.

His excellent initial shooting scores

BELOW A Warren Commission photo of Oswald

LEE HARVEY OSWALD AS A MARINE
COMMISSION EXHIBIT No. 2894

ABOVE Oswald hands out 'Hands Off Cuba' leaflets

a hardship discharge by claiming his mother needed care. He used the money to travel to the Soviet Union to try to defect but his application was refused. He made a half-hearted suicide attempt so the Soviets kept him under observation in a psychiatric unit. He was then allowed to stay because the Americans didn't believe he knew anything of interest, but, instead of working at Moscow University, Oswald was sent to Minsk as a lathe operator.

By 1961 Oswald had grown bored of his job and the dreary surroundings so he moved back to the US with Marina Prusakova and their young daughter. The Russians had realised that he had never been a CIA operative and couldn't be moulded into a Russian agent either so they let him go. When he returned to America, Oswald expected to become a media sensation but he was largely ignored.

Disillusioned with life, Oswald bought

saw him reach the rank of sharpshooter but further tests dropped him back to marksman. He was court-martialled twice, once for discharging an unauthorised handgun into his own elbow and again for fighting with the sergeant who punished him. Then, having inexplicably fired his weapon into the jungle in the Philippines, he was demoted to private.

In September 1959 Oswald received

an Italian 6.5mm Carcano bolt-action rifle and a Smith & Wesson revolver by mail order. On the night of April 10th 1963 Oswald shot at retired Major-General Edwin Walker, a vehement anti-Communist who had a following in the south. The bullet deflected off Walker's window frame and he survived with minor injuries to his arm.

(There were no suspects in this shooting until after the Kennedy assassination. Marina testified to the Warren Commission that her husband believed Walker to be a fascist and that he'd confessed to the attempt on the general's life. The bullet found in Walker's office was too badly damaged for most forensic tests but neutron activation analysis – a process for assessing the concentrations of various elements in the atomic nucleus – later concluded that it was extremely likely the bullet was made by the same manufacturer and fired by the same rifle as that used in the Kennedy assassination.)

Oswald returned to New Orleans, set up a Fair Play for Cuba office and began distributing leaflets backing Fidel Castro. He then tried to convince his wife to help him hijack a plane to Cuba but Marina was pregnant with their second child and thought the plan ridiculous. Soon afterwards, Oswald arrived in Mexico City where he applied for a visa to the Soviet Union via Cuba. He was eventually given permission to enter Cuba but decided instead to return to Dallas.

With his life going nowhere, he applied for a job at the Texas School Book Depository. Just before Kennedy arrived in Dallas, the motorcade route was announced: it passed directly in front of the book depository. On November 22nd, Oswald left $170 and his wedding ring with Marina and turned up for work with a long, heavy package, which he said contained curtain rods. Oswald was seen by several co-workers on the first floor of the depository in the hour before the shooting and then on the sixth floor at 11.55am.

Ninety seconds after the assassination Oswald was spotted in the second-floor lunchroom by police officer Marrion Baker. Baker drew his gun and approached Oswald but building manager Roy Truly intervened and said that Oswald worked at the depository. Neither man thought Oswald looked in the least bit flustered and he was

NEW ORLEANS, LA.
112 723
8   9   63

allowed to leave the building by the front entrance. When witnesses came forward to say that they had heard shots from the sixth floor and Oswald was the only employee missing, the police manhunt began.

At 12.40pm Oswald took a bus and taxi to his room on North Beckley Avenue. The housekeeper said he only stayed for a few moments before leaving. A few minutes later, Oswald was approached by Dallas Patrolman J D Tippit who had heard the description of the man wanted in connection with the assassination. As soon as he climbed out of his car, Tippit was shot four times.

Several witnesses heard the shooting and saw a man running from the scene with a gun. When Oswald slipped into the Texas Theatre without paying, the clerk called the police and they arrived at 1.45pm.

Oswald was surrounded on the upper balcony and was eventually disarmed and led from the theatre. He was taken to the police department and questioned about the Tippit shooting by Jim Leavelle. When Captain J W Fritz heard who they had in custody, he recognized him as the man missing

from the book depository and Oswald was booked for both murders. He was questioned several times over the next two days but he stuck to the curtain-rod story.

Two days after the shootings, Oswald was being led through the basement of the police department by Leavelle when Jack Ruby, a nightclub owner and small-time criminal who was known to have links within the police department and with the Mafia, shot Oswald in the lower

LEFT Oswald's mugshot following his arrest for fighting with Carlos Bringuier

ABOVE Oswald is led from the Texas Theatre after his capture

ABOVE Jack Ruby shoots Oswald before Jim Leavelle (left) can react

so he couldn't divulge information about organised crime to the police. Ruby maintained until his death in 1967, however, that he had shot Oswald to spare Jackie the agony of sitting through his trial, and because Oswald had killed his president.

The case against Oswald remains convincing: he had bought a Carcano rifle and a revolver before the assassination; witnesses saw a man lean out of the sixth floor window and fire three shots at the motorcade; three spent cartridges were found near the gun in the depository; the gun and surrounding boxes had Oswald's palm prints on them; the improvised paper bag he'd been seen with that morning was also found near the sniper's nest; more than half of the people in Dealey Plaza said all three shots originated from the book depository; ballistic and forensic analysis of Kennedy's gunshot

left chest. He was pronounced dead at Parkland Memorial Hospital just after 1pm.

The murder was captured live on television and has given rise to hundreds of conspiracy theories, most of which centre around Ruby silencing Oswald

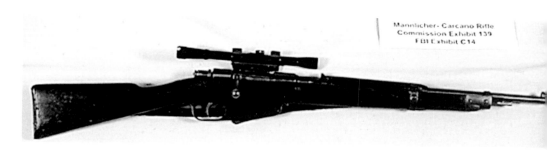

ABOVE The Carcano rifle bought by Oswald

LEFT A Smith & Wesson Model 10 of the type used to kill Officer Tippit

wounds confirm that the shots were fired from the sixth floor of the depository; a bullet found on Governor Connally's hospital gurney and two fragments from the presidential limousine were matched to the rifle; fibres on the rifle were matched with Oswald's shirt, and his hands had traces of firearms residue on them; Oswald was positively identified by nine independent witnesses as being the killer of J D Tippit; the cartridge cases found at the second murder scene belonged to Oswald's revolver – which was on him when he was arrested – to the exclusion of all other weapons; and his wife, Marina, insisted that she had taken the photos of Oswald with the murder weapons and that the pictures could not have been faked.

Independent investigations into the shooting by the Warren Commission, Attorney General Robert Kennedy, J Edgar Hoover at the FBI, John McCone

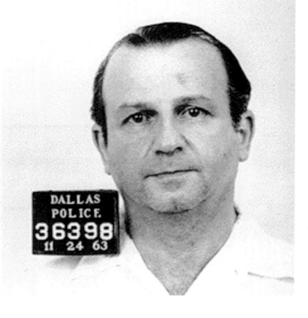

at the CIA and James Rowley of the Secret Service (amongst others) all concluded that Oswald acted alone and that he was driven by a hatred of his country and its society, and an overwhelming desire to be remembered as a person of consequence.

THE WARREN COMMISSION

In the aftermath of the assassination and the subsequent murder of Lee Harvey Oswald, President Johnson knew he had to provide the public with answers. He appointed Chief Justice Earl Warren to head up the investigation so that rumours of foreign involvement could be dispelled.

The pressure to deliver a report in good time was enormous; the longer it took to investigate, the more time the theories had to evolve. When the report was delivered in September 1964, it said that the shots that had killed Kennedy

and injured Governor Connally were fired from the sixth floor of the book depository. It based this assumption on eyewitness testimony from Howard Brennan and Amos Euins, both of whom had seen a man lean out of the window and fire at the motorcade; the fact that the bullet found on Connally's stretcher matched the Carcano rifle found in the depository to the exclusion of all other weapons; the three used cartridges found in the sniper's nest also matched the rifle; the limousine's windshield was struck on the inside by a bullet fragment; and the nature of the wounds to both men indicated the bullets were fired from above, behind and slightly to the right of the motorcade.

Having thoroughly investigated Oswald's connections with the Soviet Union; the Fair Play for Cuba Committee; the Socialist Workers' Party; the Communist Party, USA; and his meetings with contacts at the Russian and Cuban embassies in Mexico City; the FBI; the CIA; and any other governmental agency, the commission blamed Oswald alone for the assassination.

It cited his deep-rooted resentment of authority, his inability to form close relationships, his rejection of society, his urge to forge a place in history to mask his daily shortcomings and failures in civilian life, and his commitment to antagonising the US by declaring himself a Marxist as his motives for carrying out the assassination, and it also said that the attempt on Walker's life proved that he had the capacity for violence and the mindset of a man capable of killing.

There was general acceptance of the commission's findings from the media but an immediate outcry from the public. Despite the overwhelming evidence, the American people didn't believe it was possible for Oswald to have acted alone, and several alternate theories sprang up after inconsistencies were unearthed in the initial report: a third of all the witnesses in the plaza believed the shots came from the grassy knoll to the front and to the right of the motorcade; seven people claimed to have seen smoke from the stockade fence on the knoll and an eighth said he smelled gunpowder; Gordon Arnold said his cine camera, which had captured the assassination from behind the picket fence on the knoll, was confiscated by two policemen immediately afterwards; some of the president's autopsy

photographs were not released and several experts claimed the photos that were released were doctored; the limousine was cleaned before detailed forensic analysis could be carried out; many people believe that the first shot to strike Kennedy could not also have been responsible for Governor Connally's

RIGHT American
politician and US
senator Robert
F Kennedy

injuries, which suggests there were at least two assassins; initial police reports stated that the weapon found in the depository was a 7.65 Mauser, not a 6.5 Carcano; the House Select Committee on Assassinations concluded that four shots had been fired – with one coming from the grassy knoll – and that acoustic evidence confirmed this; several people claimed at least one shot had been fired from the roof of the neighbouring Dal-Tex Building; former marine colleagues of Oswald thought he was a lousy shot; the rifle had suspect telescopic sights; and several police marksmen could not replicate the three shots in the 5.6 seconds stipulated by the Warren Commission.

More evidence for multiple shooters came from Lee Bowers who was in a railroad tower overlooking the yard behind the grassy knoll. He said he saw two men on the knoll, that one of them was wearing a dark jacket, and that one or more of the shots could have been fired from this position, although the echo meant that he also considered the book depository as being the origin of the shots. The famous film of the assassination taken by Abraham Zapruder appears to show Kennedy's head being snapped back and to the left, which could suggest he was hit by a shot from the front right.

So although the evidence against Oswald may have been strong and every mock trial conducted since the assassination found him guilty, a number of organisations also had motives for killing Kennedy.

ORGANISED CRIME

Since the late 1950s, JFK and his brother, Robert, had been clamping down on organised crime. They targeted Carlos Marcello in Louisiana in particular. Robert Kennedy had twice deported Marcello and the crime boss was seething with resentment so he made these threats against Bobby and JFK: "A dog will still bite you if you cut off its tail, whereas if you cut off the dog's head, the tail will no longer wag." The mob was also angered by the fact that Kennedy's father had allegedly used their cash from bootlegged alcohol during Prohibition to get John elected and, now that the family was in power, Bobby was biting the hand that had fed them by targeting organised crime.

Conspiracy theorists point to failed

assassination attempts by Thomas Vallee in Chicago and Gilberto Lopez in Tampa as evidence that the mob was going to use a patsy to kill Kennedy. Oswald was recruited for the last opportunity in Dallas, but he would have to be silenced, which is where Jack Ruby enters the picture.

Four men who had been seen with rifles were put under surveillance in Chicago and the threat was serious enough for the Secret Service to cancel Kennedy's visit, although Vallee, who didn't have any connection with the men and was known to have mental health problems, was later released. It's likely that the stash of ammunition and weapons found at his house was pure coincidence. The FBI tip off to the Secret Service ensured that no assassination attempt took place. Gilberto Lopez suffered epileptic seizures and was trying to return to his home in Cuba so he also seems an unlikely candidate to assassinate the president or take the fall as a patsy.

There are more problems with the mob connection. If the patsies were silenced, who was supposed to silence them? Ruby never spoke of a link with organised crime. Also, if the Mafia was linked with the assassination beyond doubt, then surely Bobby Kennedy would have clamped down even harder.

The final nail in the coffin for mob involvement is the fact that despite the clampdown the Mafia needed Kennedy. The crime bosses believed he was trying to remove Castro and they were desperate to restart their lucrative gambling, drug and smuggling businesses in Havana. Kennedy was far more important to them than Castro and they needed him alive if the CIA was to carry out any future coup in Cuba. With Castro out of the way, they could resume operations.

FIDEL CASTRO

Castro was presiding over a Communist government that was allied with the Soviet Union. From 1959 he oversaw the import of Russian nuclear missiles that were soon pointing at the United States. When American U-2 spy planes discovered the missile sites matters came to a head during the Cuban Missile Crisis. It was no secret that the Eisenhower and Kennedy administrations were concerned about the threat and were determined to remove Castro via a variety of measures, some peaceful and legitimate, others illicit and overtly aggressive.

Kennedy armed 1,400 dissidents who sailed for Cuba from Nicaragua while eight B-26s bombed airfields inland. Castro didn't anticipate an amphibious landing at the Bay of Pigs and the coast was poorly defended. The CIA had hoped that the rebels

LEFT It is widely reputed that during the Kennedy administration the CIA recruited Sam Giancana and other mobsters to assassinate Cuban president Fidel Castro

BELOW Castro (right) enters Havana in 1959

on the island would now rise up and overthrow Castro but many defected, allowing Castro to launch an effective counter offensive. Kennedy refused to step in and abandoned the rebels. It was a triumph for the Cuban leader and a disaster for Kennedy because it gave Castro a compelling motive to strike back. The Warren Commission completely overlooked the possible link between Castro and the assassination, however.

In the mid-1970s the House Select Committee on Assassinations re-examined the evidence and even visited Castro in Havana. G Robert Blakey suggested to the Cuban president that he might have been involved but Castro

denied the accusation with a strong argument: it would have given the US the perfect excuse to invade Cuba again, something he had worked his entire life to avoid.

On balance, it is certainly possible that Castro ordered Kennedy's assassination but the reality was quite different. Having forced Khrushchev into backing down during the missile crisis, Kennedy's advisors urged him to build bridges with Castro. Kennedy asked TV personality Lisa Howard and French reporter Jean Daniel to extend olive branches to the Cuban leader. And three days before the assassination, Kennedy delivered a speech promising to promote ties with Cuba. Castro was enthusiastic

LITTLE BOOK OF **CONSPIRACY THEORIES**

about a warming of the relationship because he was disappointed with the involvement of the Russians on the island, and he was devastated when news of the assassination came through. This rules out his involvement in the shooting in Dallas.

THE RUSSIANS

There are essentially two theories about Soviet involvement in the Kennedy assassination, the first being that the KGB carried out the shooting, and the second that they coerced Oswald into pulling the trigger.

The US government was extremely suspicious of the Soviet regime in the early 1960s and they were worried that a possible first strike against America would involve removing the president and vice-president. (This was why Lyndon Johnson was so eager to board Air Force One in the aftermath of the assassination.)

Oswald visited the Russian Embassy in Mexico in October claiming that his life was being made unbearable by the FBI surveillance and that he wanted to return to the Soviet Union. His application was denied so he headed for Dallas instead.

At least this is the official version given by Oleg Nechiporenko, one of the diplomats who interviewed Oswald. But it doesn't tally with the stories given by Pavel Yatskov and Valeri Kostikov who were also present. All three have since been outed as members of the KGB. Indeed, according to the CIA, Kostikov specialised in sabotage and assassination.

Kennedy had stood up to the Russians during the Cuban Missile Crisis and this humiliated the Soviet leadership. Whether Nikita Khrushchev knew of a plot to target Kennedy or if a hard-line Stalinist element went behind his back isn't clear but the theory goes that the hardliners wanted war with the Americans or for Kennedy to back down.

A brilliant spy called Ivan Serov had overseen the displacement and liquidation of enemies of the state during the Second World War, so Khrushchev appointed him head of the KGB in 1954 and head of military intelligence (the GRU) five years later. Serov had powerful allies in the shape of Yuri Andropov and Vladimir Kryuchkov, and many believe it was these three who planned the assassination.

Serov contacted Kostikov and tried to convince him that the assassination was officially sanctioned by the Kremlin. Indeed, many have asked why a man of so little importance like Oswald would have been granted an audience in Mexico with Kostikov and two other senior diplomats. The reason was that Oswald was being recruited for the assassination. The theory gained credibility when it emerged that the 'diplomats' sent a telegram to Moscow immediately after meeting Oswald.

J Edgar Hoover passed President Johnson information on Oswald in the weeks before the assassination, which convinced him that the Soviets were behind a plot to kill Kennedy. When he heard that Oswald had lived in Russia, was under FBI surveillance and had tried to enter Cuba, Johnson was appalled, and this information naturally reinforced his opinion that there was a conspiracy afoot

Robert Holmes, author of *Spy Like No Other*, believes that of all the conspiracy theories this one is the most likely as it is credible, easily implementable and fits with most of the circumstantial and forensic evidence. Oswald carried out the shooting alone but he was working for a rogue faction within the KGB.

If Oswald wasn't involved and had merely been framed for the shooting, however, could KGB agents have carried out the assassination? There is no doubt that Khrushchev had been humiliated during the missile crisis, but was this a powerful enough motive to kill the president? The Warren Commission didn't believe there was a shred of evidence implicating the Russians, but recently released files hinted at the KGB targeting international leaders like Imre Nagy in Hungary, Gheorghui-Dej in Romania, Jan Masaryk in Czechoslovakia, the Shah of Iran, Mao Tse-tung and President Kennedy.

Although there will always be proponents of the Soviet conspiracy, and it does seem the most plausible given Oswald's connections and his self-professed Marxism, the motivation provides the major stumbling block. Kennedy may have embarrassed Krushchev but the two men respected one another and neither wanted nuclear war, something a first strike at Kennedy could have provoked.

THE CIA AND THE FBI

In 2003, a poll showed that nearly a fifth of Americans believed Vice-President Lyndon Johnson and the country's security services were involved in the Kennedy assassination. It was no secret that the men disliked one another because the vice-president thought Kennedy was going to drop him in the build-up to the 1964 election.

Authors Joachim Joesten and Barr McClellan accused Johnson and the Dallas oligarchy, along with the security services, of plotting the assassination because they were worried about Kennedy changing the oil depletion allowance, which would cost them $100 million. They supposedly paid Johnson's associate Malcolm Wallace to fire at the motorcade from the depository. Indeed, one of the partial fingerprints found in the sniper's nest apparently belonged to Wallace even though he'd never been in the building.

Even Doctor Charles Crenshaw, who had tried to save both Kennedy and Oswald at Parkland Hospital, suggested that Johnson wanted details of the assassination covered up. He said that the new president had asked for a full confession from Oswald because he wanted the American people to believe he'd acted alone. Oswald, of course, was mortally wounded and was in no condition to give a statement.

After the disastrous Bay of Pigs

BELOW Allen Dulles

invasion, Kennedy blamed the CIA for a lack of intelligence. He and Bobby felt there was distrust between them and the agency so they sacked Allen Dulles in 1961. Johnson was staunchly behind the CIA and could barely disguise his hatred of Kennedy so he apparently organised the hit so he could assume the presidency, keep the CIA well funded and allow it to continue its covert operations.

Three 'tramps' in the plaza were identified by conspiracy theorists as E Howard Hunt, a CIA station chief who apparently gave a deathbed confession over his and Johnson's involvement in 2007; CIA agent Frank Sturgis, who was also involved in the Bay of Pigs invasion and who was said to be one of the gunmen; and Chauncey Holt, a man claiming to be a double agent for both the CIA and the Mafia. Hunt also claimed Agent David Morales and an unnamed French assassin were involved, the latter firing at the motorcade from the grassy knoll.

Photos of the three tramps bear a surprising resemblance to Hunt, Sturgis and Holt but the men who had made the comparisons – assassination researchers Alan Weberman and Michael Canfield – had no formal training in photographic identification, and the FBI's department of photo-identification and analysis concluded that none of the tramps was Hunt or Sturgis.

The evidence against Johnson, the CIA and the FBI is barely credible. Although Kennedy had a number of disagreements with the agency, Deputy Director John Hegerson felt that their relationship was better than that which

BELOW Frank Sturgis and Tramp B were supposed to be one and the same person

STURGIS

TRAMP B

ABOVE Castro's troops at Playa de Citron after successfully repelling the US-backed invasion of the Bay of Pigs

had been nurtured under Eisenhower.

The accusations levelled at Johnson in particular are unfounded. The new president was convinced that Castro was responsible but he was powerless to act in case tension with the Soviet Union escalated. So although Johnson wasn't involved, he did try to cover up what he believed was the truth about Castro's part in the shooting. His biographer, Robert Caro, found no evidence from his exhaustive research that Johnson had any involvement in the assassination either, a fact those conspiracy theorists overlook having not done the research themselves.

So if we conclude that Oswald was in the book depository, was he acting alone?

THE SINGLE BULLET THEORY

One of the most contentious issues surrounding the assassination involves the bullets themselves. How many were fired, from where did they originate, and who or what did they hit? Most witnesses in the plaza – including Governor Connally who was an experienced hunter – counted three shots. In all, 132 of 178 witnesses, an overwhelming majority, said they heard exactly three shots and that there was a noticeable pause after the first shot, while the last two were much closer together.

This gives rise to several different theories about the shooting, one of which (the official Warren Commission version) states that the first shot missed, while the second struck Kennedy in the upper back and, having passed through his body, then caused all the injuries to Connally in the seat in front. This is known as the single bullet theory. The third bullet then struck Kennedy in the head. The first shot, which the commission said missed the motorcade, has never been satisfactorily accounted for.

One of the conspiracy theories states that the initial injury to Kennedy and the wounds to Connally could not have been caused by the same bullet as the two men don't appear to react at the same time on the Zapruder film. This has given rise to the magic bullet theory, magic because it apparently entered too low in Kennedy's back to exit his throat, then waited in mid-air before striking Connally in the back and changing course several times to inflict all of his injuries. There's little doubt that the third shot struck Kennedy in the head, but some argue that it might have happened at exactly the same time as a fourth shot was fired from the grassy knoll.

The Warren Commission eventually decided that a single bullet had struck both Kennedy's upper torso and Connally's back, but they hadn't initially reached this conclusion. When examining the Zapruder film, which had a frame speed of 18.3 per second, they decided that Kennedy first reacted to the impact of a bullet between frames 225 and 226. Connally, on the other hand, didn't seem to react until around frame 235. Ten frames of the film corresponded to only just over half a second, nowhere near enough time for the shooter to reload, aim and fire

CE 399

FBI C1

National Archives

ABOVE A tiny hole can be seen in the bottom right hand corner of the traffic light in this FBI photo. It might help explain what happened to the first, missed, shot

the seats in the car, the injury trajectories through the president and Connally's bodies aligned very closely, providing the bullet had been fired between frames 207 and 240 when Connally's body was in the right position.

Three agents found the single impact theory improbable because of the relatively pristine condition of the bullet when it was found on Connally's hospital gurney, even though the bullet was matched to the rifle in the book depository to the exclusion of all other weapons.

As any high-powered rifle bullet striking both men would have taken less than a hundredth of a second to pass between them, it's hard to explain why both men don't appear to react at the same time. The conspiracy theorists believe this is incontrovertible evidence that there must have been more than one gunman, despite the forensic evidence pointing to the bullets coming from the Carcano in the depository.

Some theorists believe that the fatal shot was fired from a storm drain in the pavement on Elm Street in front of the limousine, but when *Unsolved History* tried to recreate the shot from this position, the president wouldn't even

accurately. The FBI had already tested the rifle and concluded that it took at least 2.3 seconds (42 frames) to recycle the weapon. They therefore agreed with the commission's initial findings that there must have been at least two snipers in the plaza.

However, when the FBI re-enacted the shooting in May 1964 they found that because of the actual positions of

have been visible. Even more suggest that shots came from the drains on top of the triple underpass or from the plaza's southern knoll. The south end of the underpass can immediately be ruled out because the drain hadn't been installed by November 1963, and there was no direct line of sight to Kennedy for the fatal shot. The same is true from the knoll. The north side of the underpass offered a shot at the president's head but there were trees and people in the line of fire and a sniper would have been unlikely to have fired from this position.

ABOVE When questioned, Amos Euins said he heard the first shot when the limousine had just passed beneath the traffic signals. The ghost image shows where the limousine was when Zapruder started filming again

Railroad employees on the underpass were all interviewed after the shooting and they insisted they saw no one and nothing unusual. This rules out the triple underpass as a vantage point for a sniper.

The second floor of the Dal-Tex building was also named as a potential vantage point but, when the presidential limousine was at the position of the two shots that definitely struck the occupants, there was no direct route to Connally's back, meaning the single bullet theory from the book depository was infinitely more likely than a 'magic' bullet from elsewhere.

On balance, the ballistic evidence suggests that the first shot from the depository probably occurred earlier than most people thought (when Zapruder wasn't filming). Because it missed, what happened to it remained a mystery until a new investigation into the shooting by Max Holland in 2011 discovered that it almost certainly struck the traffic light assembly above the corner of Houston and Elm (a hole can be seen in the lights in the FBI's photographs of the crime scene) and that it disintegrated and ricocheted down the street where fragments struck the curb and injured James Tague.

The second shot was probably fired at Zapruder during frame 221. It struck Kennedy two inches to the right of his spine in his upper back, then passed through his neck and exited out of his throat just below his Adam's apple. It then began tumbling before striking Governor Connally below his right armpit, passing through his chest and exiting below his right nipple (frame 223). The entrance wound in Connally's back provided the strongest possible evidence for one shooter because it was elongated. Bullets invariably tumble only having already struck something else. If it had struck the governor first, it would have made a small entrance hole like the one in Kennedy's back. The fact that it had already passed through Kennedy's body and had begun tumbling is the only possible explanation for the governor's lateral entrance wound.

Close analysis of the digitally re-mastered Zapruder film shows the lapel on Connally's jacket puffing out in this frame so this was when the bullet exited the governor's chest. A couple of frames later, both the governor and Kennedy react in unison to the impact of a single

ABOVE The limousine is cleaned outside the hospital

bullet, much earlier in Connally's case than had previously been believed. It then entered and exited his wrist before lodging shallowly in his thigh. When he was undressed in the hospital, the bullet was dislodged and was found on the stretcher.

Opponents of the single bullet theory still refuse to accept that the bullet could be in such good condition having done so much damage, but tests done at the time by the Warren Commission and many more since have proved that these bullets *can* survive with only slight flattening when they hit skin layers and ballistics gel, as well as when they strike harder substances like wood and bone.

The third, fatal, shot hit Kennedy at frame 313, or approximately five seconds after the second shot. The

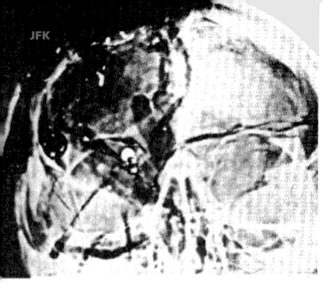

JFK

the physics of the impact (the skull blow out causes an equal and opposite reaction) and a stiffening of the body due to massive nerve damage do contribute to a secondary movement to the left rear. A re-enactment by British sniper Michael Yardley for the program *Unsolved History: Inside the Target Car* replicated the results with a shot from the position of the sixth floor window in the depository. Yardley also found that a shot from the front right on the knoll would have passed through Kennedy's head and struck Jackie, which clearly did not happen.

The photos from the autopsy are readily available, and almost all of the experts who have examined them believe them to be real and unaltered, so it is difficult to side with the conspiracy theorists. The entry wounds to the president's back and to the rear of the skull, the blow-out on the right hand side of the head above the ear and the X-rays provide conclusive evidence that Kennedy was struck twice, with one bullet passing through his back and exiting his throat, and the second entering the rear of his head. Both were fired from the sixth floor of the Texas School Book Depository.

sniper therefore probably had as much as 11 seconds in which to take the three shots, not the six seconds (or fewer) claimed by most conspiracy theorists.

Although it appears that Kennedy's head is snapped back and to the left, Dale Myers's award-winning animation of the assassination, which was based on the Zapruder film, shows his head initially moving forward by up to two inches (five cm). When the side of Kennedy's skull blows out from the impact, his head then rolls to the left. This is again consistent with a shot from the rear, not from the front as

CONCLUSION

There is no doubt that the Kennedy assassination will divide opinion for the foreseeable future. Although some of the conspiracy theories raise important points, most are not based on demonstrable fact, solid science or the overwhelming circumstantial and forensic evidence. A classic case in point is the Oliver Stone film *JFK*, which reignited interest in the event and brought his version of it to a wider audience, but it completely distorts the truth and uses little forensic and ballistic evidence.

Stone suggests that there were a number of sinister happenings in New Orleans, including David Ferrie's 'confession', Oswald printing Fair Play for Cuba leaflets and then handing them out while Clay Shaw looks on, and Richard Helms admitting that Shaw worked for the CIA. Stone, unfortunately, did not base any of these incidents on real events: Ferrie never confessed and always denied any knowledge of Oswald or the assassination plot; the leaflets Oswald handed out were not printed by him; and Helms never claimed that Shaw

worked for the CIA.

Stone also took liberties with the events themselves, as well as the witness reports from Dealey Plaza: he puts Kennedy and Connally in seats that are the same height and alignment,

BELOW President John Fitzgerald Kennedy in 1960

ABOVE Portrait of John Fitzgerald Kennedy

appears on the grassy knoll, but no one reported this; Jim Garrison (played by Kevin Costner) claims that 51 people heard shots from the knoll but even the advocates of the many theories have managed to identify only around 20; in the film, Bill Newman says the shots came from the stockade fence on the knoll, whereas he actually believed the shots came from the mall behind him; it's claimed that if the sniper was Oswald, he couldn't have fired the last shot, stashed the rifle and been seen 90 seconds later in the lunchroom completely unflustered, but the trip through the depository only takes 45 seconds at walking pace; and Lyndon Johnson apparently asks for the limo filled with bullet holes to be refurbished, but the bullet strike to the windshield and damage to the chrome can be seen in the national archives. (This list of factual inaccuracies is nowhere near exhaustive.)

but Connally was sitting in a lowered inboard jump-seat that was offset from the president's; he has Jackie pulling Kennedy down into the car to make way for the shot that hits Connally, but this does not happen in the Zapruder film; the entry wound in Kennedy's back and the exit wound in his neck are incorrectly positioned; a cloud of smoke

So although it is certainly possible that there were three or more snipers in the plaza, and it's equally possible that the mob, Russians, Cubans or intelligence agencies were somehow involved, it's

much more likely that Oswald alone was responsible. This is what the facts and not the Hollywood misinterpretation or the conspiracy theories suggest. The film, of course, reached a global audience of millions and only served to inflate misguided opinion.

Also, how is it possible for a government to keep evidence suppressed or kill off all the important witnesses without someone blowing the whistle? It's impossible for politicians to keep secrets for more than a few minutes so how could the enormous number of people required by each theory manage to keep quiet for half a century? No alternative has stood up to detailed analysis by credible investigators. Witness testimony can often be discredited (as was the acoustic evidence) and honest clerical errors can be made during the investigation but, because they cloud the issue, the theories refuse to die.

Why couldn't a disillusioned and mentally unstable man have ordered a rifle, taken it to work and shot someone? Just because that person was the most powerful man on Earth and he was supposed to be protected by the Secret Service doesn't necessarily mean that a huge conspiracy was involved in the assassination. We want there to be equilibrium, with the president and his entourage on one side, and the killer with backing from a vast network on the other because then the events seem more plausible, but it's perfectly possible for Oswald to have acted alone and the vast majority of the evidence backs this up. His brother, Robert, knew Oswald better than anyone, and he has always maintained Lee's guilt, and that he acted alone.

The fact remains that Oswald had the means, motive and opportunity to carry out the assassination, and it was he who pulled the trigger.

Chapter 2

Aliens and UFOs

The term **unidentified flying object, or UFO, covers a broad range of sightings of mysterious objects in the sky. Because the observer can't always explain the sightings, many of these events are attributed to alien spacecraft visiting us from other worlds.**

Contrary to popular belief and what we read in the newspapers, our Voyager spacecraft haven't really left the solar system because the sun's influence – such as its gravitational field and the radiation it emits – extends beyond the comets and asteroids in the Oort Cloud two light years away. Voyager is around 18 light *hours* away from Earth, nowhere near the outer reaches of the solar system. Indeed it will probably take the craft another 30,000 years to reach true interstellar space, so by our standards it seems unlikely that anyone or anything could survive such enormous interplanetary undertakings, and indeed most UFO sightings can be explained rationally. However, once unusual or secret military aircraft, strange cloud formations, weather balloons, meteorites, satellites, planets, celebratory Chinese lanterns and hoaxes have been ruled out, a small percentage of sightings remain difficult to explain and few investigations lead to the publication of credible scientific papers.

But this only rouses the conspiracy theorists who believe our governments are covering up the truth...

UFOs may have only become part of popular culture in the last half-century or so but many ancient cultures appear

to have chronicled alien visitations in their artwork. Granite carvings dating from 45,000BC in Hunan in Asia, for example, appear to show humans gazing at a series of cylindrical objects hovering in the sky. Rock carvings in Peru from 11,000BC, at Tassili in the Sahara from 6,000BC and from Nambu in Africa from around 4,300BC all depict figures with large, helmet-like heads, and some appear to be wearing spacesuits similar to those worn by modern astronauts.

Early Aboriginal art as well as paintings from a 3,000-year-old Japanese culture also seem to show spacemen.

Texts from ancient India dating back 5,000 years, and an Egyptian papyrus from 1504BC, describe circles of fire coming from the sky that were brighter than the sun, and there are even references to UFOs in the Bible and ancient Greek and Roman scripts. Many people also believe that the Nazca Lines in Peru (enormous carvings of

ABOVE
The Hummingbird outline of the Nazca Lines

Anno M. D. LXI An dem XIIII. tag Aprillis zu morgens
zwischen sům zehen tag vnd dem garauff/das ist zu morgens zwischen 4 vnd
5 auff der kleinen vhr/ist ein sehr erschröcklich gesicht an der Son wie sie im
auffgang gewesen erschinnen/vnd zu Nůrmberg in der Stat vnd vor dem
vber vnd auff dem Land von vielen mans vnd weybs personen gesehen worden. Erstlich ist die Sonn mit zweyen blut farben halb runden strichē/gleichsermig wie
der Monn im abnemen/mitten durch die Sonne erschinnen vnd gesehen worden/vnd inn
der Sonne/oben/vnten/ Vnd auch seben seytten blut farbe/vnd eines theyls klösliche oder
Eysen farbe auch schwartz farb runde Kugel gestanden/ Desselben gleichen auff bayden
seytten vnd ringschweben vmb die Sonne herumb/sein solche blut rote/vnd der andern kugel
in anzal viel/etwo drey ins die lenge/vnter weylen vier im einem Quatrangel/auch etliche
ainzig gestanden/Vnd zwischen solchen Kugeln sein auch etliche blutfarbe Creütz gesehen/
vnd zwischen solchen Creützen vnd Kugeln sein blutfarbe streymen binden dick/ Vnd vom
hinauff / etwas geschmeydiger als bocken rböl/Allenthalben mit ein vermischt gewesen/
sampt vnter andern zweyen grossen rören/eines zur rechten/vnd des ander zur lincken hande/
stehent/in welchen kleinen vnd grossen Ror/zu begreyssen/auch vier vnd mehr kugel gewesen.
Dieses alles hat mit einander anzusehen zu streyten/sein die kugel so erschlich in der Son ge-
wesen/herauff als fiels zu beyden seytten gestanden/gefaren/so sein die so herausen ge-
sen/sampt den kugeln auff den klein vnd grossen Rорn/im die Sonne hinein gefaren/zu dem

haben die Roteßen so sehr alle die kugel vnter einander gefaren/vnd hefftig alles miteinander geschittet vnd/gefochten/bey einer guten stundt/ Vnd wie der Streyt das ein weyl inn
die Sonne hinein/vnd widerumb heraus am hefftigsten bin vnd her gefarē/sich der maß-
sen miteinander abgenart/Ist es alles wie obverzeychnet ober den Sonnen/vom Hymel
herab auff die erden gleich alle ob es alles Brenne gefallen/vnd mit einem grossen dampff
beronten auff der Erden allgemach vergangen. Nach solchem allen ist auch gleichsörmig
einem schwartzen Speer/der schaft vom auffgang/ Vnd die spitzen zum Nidergang inn
grosser dick vnd leng gesehen worden. Was aber solche zeychen bedeuten/ist Gott allein
wissent/dieweyl wir aber kurtz auffenander/souil vnd mancherley zeychen am Hymel ba-
ben/die vns der Allmechtige Gott/von vnsers sindlichen lebens/damit er vns gern zur Buß
reytzen vnd locken wil/erscheinen last/so sein wir leyder so vndanckbar/das wir solche hohe
zeychen vnd Wunderwerck Gottes verachten/ Auch spelich davon reden/ vnd inn winde
schlagen/Zvsösongenes werde vns Gott vmb vnserer vndanckbareyt/allen sein schröck-
liche straff senden/Jedoch werden solche die Gotsfürchtigen in kainen weg verachten/son-
der alle diese trewe warnung jres gnedigen Vatters im Hymel behertzigen/jr Leben bes-
sen/Gott trewlich bitten/Das er seinen billigen zorn/sampt dem wol verdienten straff von
vns woll abwenden/Damit wir alle seine kinder hie zeytlich/vnd dort ewig leben mögen/
darzu vns Gott allen wölle helffen/Amen.

§ Bey Hanns Glaser Briefftmaler/zu Nürmberg.

animals that can only be seen from the air), which date back at least 5,000 years, can only have been created by aliens.

Chinese astronomers noticed an unusual object in the night sky 2,500 years ago. They saw it as a religious omen, although today we believe it was probably Halley's Comet. The comet reappears every 76 years or so, so it crops up regularly as a UFO across all cultures and peoples of the world. The Chinese also documented a large 'guest star' in 1054, so called because it could be seen in the sky, night and day, for two years.

We now know this was a result of the supernova explosion that formed the Crab Nebula, which has become the most studied astronomical entity outside our solar system, but the Shen Kuo (a government official in the 11th century) sighting is not so easily explained.

He recorded similar stories from several eyewitnesses in Yangzhou, each of whom claimed to have seen a flying object that shone brilliant lights from its open doors before disappearing at extreme speeds. In an age before mechanical technology, this sighting is particularly difficult to explain.

Indeed, there were many more cases of unusual objects recorded in the skies during the Middle Ages, an event at Nuremburg in 1561 providing us with several eyewitness accounts. Residents described an hour-long battle between oddly shaped craft that resulted in a crash outside the city. News notices and engravings of the event survive in the Wickiana Collection in Zurich.

It was not until 1878 in Denison, Texas, that the words 'flying saucer' entered our language. Farmer John Martin contacted his local newspaper to say that he'd seen a balloon-like object about the size of a saucer flying at 'wonderful speed' (this type of sighting became more common as man took to the air during the First World War).

In 1908 an enormous explosion shook the ground at Tunguska in central Russia, but it took until 1921 before an expedition finally made it to the site. More than 830 square miles of forest had been flattened by the blast but there was no impact crater. Based on a fictional account of the incident by Alexander Kasantsev in 1946, UFO believers claim this was because an enormous extraterrestrial craft exploded in the upper atmosphere. It's more likely,

LEFT A depiction of the aerial battle above Nuremburg in 1561

however, that a meteorite or comet 30-50 metres across blew itself apart five miles above the ground. (In 2013, a meteor exploded above Chelyabinsk in Russia with the energy of half a million tons of TNT. More than a thousand people were injured by the shockwave.)

In 1917 more than 30,000 people witnessed the so-called Miracle of the Sun in Fatima, Portugal. Three shepherd children had predicted that the Virgin Mary would appear at noon and thousands gathered on the hillside to wait for the miracle. After a dull morning, the sun broke through, radiating multicoloured lights and apparently spiralling towards the crowd. Outright panic was avoided but many present believed it signalled the end of the world. Scientists examining the case today cite mass hysteria and hallucinations triggered by prolonged staring at the sun as the most plausible explanation.

During WWII, Allied pilots gave the unusual metallic spheres or balls of light that appeared to follow their aircraft a name: foo fighters. They were originally thought to be secret German or Japanese weapons but Axis pilots were reporting similar sightings. Most seemed to be simple fiery spheres like Christmas-tree lights that flew in formation with the aircraft (as if they were under control) before making a few wild turns and vanishing. Despite crews from both sides trying to shoot them down, none was successful and none ever proved to be hostile, leading some people to think that it was only ball lightning, St Elmo's Fire or hallucinations caused by oxygen deprivation.

With all countries in a state of high alert during the war, it is not surprising

BELOW
The Chelyabinsk meteor blazed a fiery trail across the sky as it exploded

that there were many false alarms, such as the shelling of what was almost certainly a stray weather balloon over Los Angeles in 1942, which almost led to outright panic. After the war, several sightings made front-page news and two incidents in 1947 caught the imagination and forced the UFO phenomena into the public consciousness, where it has remained, culturally and psychologically, ever since.

Businessman Kenneth Arnold was flying his private plane near Mount Rainier in Washington when he apparently saw nine brilliant saucer- and crescent-shaped discs flying across the horizon between the mountains. His sighting was taken more seriously when an American Airlines crew spotted nine similar objects over Idaho the following week. The national press picked up on the incidents, although most tried to explain them as hallucinations or optical illusions. Some, however, believed they might have been secret weapons being tested, or, somewhat predictably, interplanetary visitors.

A few days later, the UFO phenomenon became an international sensation when Walter Haut, an army public information officer, issued a press release saying that personnel from the 509th Bomb Group had recovered parts of a flying saucer from a crash site on a farm in Roswell, New Mexico. Over the intervening years, Roswell has become the definitive UFO story. First, there were the sensational headlines. Then came the official report, which was believed for a time before being questioned by those who spotted inconsistencies in the story. When the popular conspiracy theories were denied by the military, they were accused of a cover-up and the case was eventually blown out of proportion.

ROSWELL

At the end of the Second World War, America became increasingly concerned about Stalin's imperial pretensions in Eastern Europe and the Far East. His voracious land grab led to the Cold War and heightened tension between east and west. This in turn ushered in the arms race, with both sides' frantically building nuclear weapons to deter the other from attacking. The space race came next, with the Soviet Union launching the first satellite and first man – Yuri Gagarin – into space. This

Roswell Daily Record

Leased Wire
Associated Press

RECORD PHONES
Business Office 2288
News Department
2287

RAAF Captures Flying Saucer On Ranch in Roswell Region

Claims Army Is Stacking Courts Martial

Indiana Senator Lays Protest Before Patterson

House Passes Tax Slash by Large Margin

Defeat Amendment By Demos to Remove Many from Rolls

Security Council Paves Way to Talks On Arms Reductions

No Details of Flying Disk Are Revealed

Roswell Hardware Man and Wife Report Disk Seen

Ex-King Carol Weds Mme. Lupescu

Some of Soviet Satellites May Attend Paris Meeting

Roswellians Have Differing Opinions On Flying Saucers

American League Wins All-Star Game

Miners and Operators Sign Highest Wage Pact in History

naturally concerned America because the rockets required to deliver man and machine into space meant they also had the technology to target the US with intercontinental ballistic missiles.

The uncertainty surrounding the political and military situation had everyone on edge. Kenneth Arnold's unusual sighting tapped into the national psyche and gave birth to the concept of flying saucers. The explanation favoured at the time – Arnold estimated their speed at three times the speed of sound when the sound barrier was yet to be

ABOVE The newspaper headline announced the recovery of a flying saucer

broken by Chuck Yeager – was that they must be from another world or a secret Russian project.

Two weeks later, in July 1947, William 'Mack' Brazel noticed some debris – rubber strips, tin foil, paper, scotch tape and toughened sticks – on the Foster farm where he worked. He called Sheriff Wilcox, who then contacted Major Jesse Marcel at the nearby Roswell airbase, and Marcel soon arrived to inspect the site.

Although debris was definitely recovered from the Roswell crash site, and some of it was probably taken to the top-secret Hangar 18 at Wright Field (now Wright-Patterson Air Force Base) in Ohio, the Roswell Army Airfield base commander was quick to change Haut's story of the remains coming from a flying disc to them belonging to a high-altitude weather balloon, with the bodies that had been reported at the crash site being crash test dummies. A press conference was called, the public seemed satisfied and the incident should have been consigned to history.

Early the following year, Captain Thomas Mantell, an experienced airman, crashed while apparently chasing a UFO. The large white or reflective object had been observed from Clinton County Airfield in Ohio as well as by the Kentucky Highway Patrol so four P-51 Mustangs that were already airborne were sent to investigate. The other pilots were either low on fuel or couldn't identify the object, which they believed to be small and inconsequential, so they abandoned their pursuit at 6,700 metres due to a lack of oxygen. Mantell, however, continued climbing before passing out, spiralling back to the ground and crashing fatally.

Two conventional explanations have been given for the incident: the planet Venus might have been visible and could have confused Mantell; and the navy had launched several secret Skyhook weather balloons in the area that were made from reflective aluminium, which fits with Mantell's description while he was pursuing the object. UFO proponents argue that only an advanced civilization could have engineered a device that outmanoeuvred our best technology of the time. The fact that an air force pilot died during the chase once again elevated the UFO phenomenon to the national consciousness and almost revived interest in Roswell but, despite Hollywood saturating the airwaves with

LEFT General Ramey and Colonel Dubose examine some of the wreckage from the alleged crash site

a clutch of B-movies, the crash in New Mexico seemed destined for obscurity.

But physicist and amateur ufologist Stanton Friedman wasn't convinced by the official version of events. In 1978 (no one knows why he waited 30 years) he interviewed Marcel. Marcel claimed that the military had covered up the crash and recovery of an alien spacecraft. And in 1989 mortician Glenn Dennis claimed that Brazel had found at least one body at the site and that post mortems had been carried out at the nearby airbase.

Celebrated airman Marion 'Black Mac' Magruder then told his son a

BELOW A top-secret Project Mogul balloon is prepared for launch

strange story about aliens and parts of their spacecraft arriving at Wright Field. He and another man reportedly filmed the autopsies, claiming the four-foot-tall beings had large heads, four spindly digits with no thumbs, no hair and smelled strongly of dead fish. J. Edgar Hoover was so intrigued by what he was hearing that he wrote a memo asking to be allowed access to the disc. When permission was denied, he wrote again to vent his anger at not being given more information.

Senator Barry Goldwater was interviewed about the same incident by Larry King in 1994. He outlined his attempt to be given access to Hangar 18 by Curtis LeMay but the base commander became extremely angry and told the senator never to mention the hangar again. Far from being forgotten, the case now snowballed into the most notorious UFO event in history.

In response to renewed public interest, the Secretary of the Air Force was ordered to conduct an investigation. In 1995, the first official enquiry appeared to back up the revised version of events because the US was involved in the testing of high-altitude balloons

during classified program Mogul, which was using sensitive listening devices to detect Russian nuclear tests.

A second report two years later concluded that the reports of bodies in the area were those of dummies used during parachute testing. It is also possible that a secret aircraft codenamed Silver Bug was what had actually crashed and the bodies onboard (chimps were often used in tests) were so badly burned in the resulting fire that those covering the event were confused about what they were seeing. Indeed the Laredo UFO crash near the Texas border in 1948 fits the Silver Bug hypothesis perfectly.

These projects were classified and were concealed from officials at the Roswell Army Airbase so military personnel would have been equally surprised to find bodies and/or debris.

Friedman wasn't so easily swayed

RIGHT The article in the Los Angeles Times about the UFO incident in 1942

though. Having interviewed hundreds of witnesses, he claimed that there was enough evidence to suggest that at least one spaceship had crashed at Roswell and that aliens, some of which may still have been alive, had been recovered. Others are convinced that after 30 years languishing in obscurity, it was an unusual step to resurrect the case and witness statements were distorted by time and misremembering or misinterpreting detail, something known as unintentional false memory recreation. Witness statements immediately after important events are notoriously unreliable and after three decades both military personnel and civilians undoubtedly embellished their stories.

Despite numerous books and films on the subject, opinion is still divided on the most famous UFO case of them all. But has there really been a cover up by the authorities?

UFOS AND THE WHITE HOUSE

President Franklin Roosevelt was understandably concerned about the incident over Los Angeles in 1942. He was convinced that Japanese planes were in the sky and was worried that American aircraft hadn't been scrambled and that prolonged anti-aircraft and small arms fire hadn't brought any of the enemy down. He dismissed the suggestion of UFOs out of hand but President Truman would have many more incidences to address during his tenure.

Truman was informed about Roswell by Colonel Robert Landry, whom he had appointed as his personal advisor on UFOs. The president also had to deal with the wave of sightings reported over Washington, DC in July 1952. Air traffic controllers spotted seven initial contacts on their radar on the morning of July 19th, while eyewitnesses reported seeing orange lights or discs that were moving erratically before vanishing at high speed. Personnel at Andrews Air Force Base contradicted the tower at the airport by claiming that a meteor shower was responsible. Radar specialists also suspected that unusual weather conditions such as temperature inversion could explain 'false' radar hits and sightings as mirages or meteors.

The sightings made news headlines across the country, which gained even more credence when the phenomena

THURSDAY MORNING.   **Los Angeles Times**   FEBRUARY 26, 1942. **B**

Searchlights and Anti-aircraft Guns Comb Sky During Alarm

SEEKING OUT "OBJECT"—Scores of searchlights built a wigwam of light beams over Los Angeles early yesterday morning during the alarm. This picture taken during black-out shows nine beams converging on an "object" in sky in Culver City area. The blobs of light which show at apex of beam angles were made by anti-aircraft shells.
See Story on Page 1, Part 1.   Times photo

MARKINGS—Hugh Landis of 1738 W. 43rd Place points to holes made in his car, as it stood in garage, by fragments of anti-aircraft shell that hit near by.
Times photo

BEDROOM PIERCED—Here is damage done to bedroom in home of Victor L. Norman at 2086 Easy Ave., Long Beach, when anti-aircraft shrapnel pierced dwelling.

reappeared the following weekend. This time two fighters were scrambled to intercept the objects but four of them accelerated away at speeds estimated at 7,000mph and disappeared.

President Truman was so concerned that he asked Captain Edward Ruppelt to head up Project Blue Book to look into UFO encounters. Ruppelt suggested that a temperature inversion was responsible. This is where a layer of cold air is trapped beneath a layer of warm air, which can refract light, cause unusual mirages and return false radar hits. There was even an unconfirmed report that Truman had ordered the air force to shoot down any unidentified objects. However, most aircrews saw nothing unusual in the sky over the weekends and supported the temperature inversion theory. Truman may have been persuaded that the objects themselves were illusory but he was worried that false hits and hearsay could lead to mass hysteria or panic, which might allow Russia to exploit their confusion and spread disinformation, possibly preceding an attack. So there were undoubtedly national security implications.

During President Eisenhower's eight years in the White House, UFOs became part of popular culture and after every film release sightings increased dramatically (the same was true after the release of the 1994 blockbuster *Independence Day*). Both Eisenhower and later President Kennedy were said to have witnessed sightings while at sea but they asked their crews not to mention the incidents and little of their correspondence survives today.

Johnson and Nixon were said to be interested in the phenomenon but there is no concrete evidence linking them with any sighting or covering up information. Gerald Ford was intrigued by the sightings of his constituents and launched a congressional investigation, which was then made public. Ford made further inquiries while in the White House but the air force and other authorities always denied the UFO allegations.

Jimmy Carter was the first president who openly admitted to seeing a UFO, which he claimed took place in Georgia in 1969 and was witnessed by at least 20 other people. He promised to release all governmental files on UFOs if he took office so that air force scientists and other investigators could assess what the government really knew. George

Bush Senior was Director of the CIA when Carter eventually entered the White House and he convinced Carter to renege on his promise. There can only be two credible reasons for this: UFOs existed and Bush didn't want the nation thrown into panic; or the majority of sightings were secret military projects that couldn't be made public. Carter wasn't so easily swayed, however, and he overruled Bush and oversaw the release of thousands of documents.

Reagan also witnessed UFOs on at least two occasions, and he often referred to a world uniting against a common enemy, particularly during his speech to the United Nations in 1987. Although he was clearly speaking metaphorically, he liked to include what he called his UFO fantasy in many of his public addresses. As Reagan's vice president and a former Director at Langley, George Bush Senior would have had access to the most sensitive information but few records of his interest in UFOs survive, unlike Bill Clinton who was happy to discuss the topic publicly and frequently did so. George Bush Junior threw a veil of secrecy over the topic, however, which only serves to promote rumour and innuendo. Then, in 2005, the White House was evacuated after a UFO was detected on radar approaching the building. It was eventually listed as a false alarm after an investigation concluded it was either birds or a weather balloon.

Because of the secrecy surrounding UFOs, we assume that there must be something to the story. We know that places like Area 51 in Nevada exist and we'd like to know what goes on there. It can't be coincidence that most UFO sightings occur near military installations, however. When all conventional explanations and hoaxes are ruled out, what's usually left are secret military projects, although there will always be the odd incident that can't be explained. Earthquake lights are a case in point. It was only discovered recently that unusual lights often appear in the sky before and during earthquakes. It is thought that they might be static discharges caused by subterranean friction but it reminds us that our planet still has plenty of surprises. The difference between these and possible alien sightings, however, is they are or soon will be explicable by conventional rather than pseudoscience.

AREA 51

The military base at Groom Lake in Nevada is one of the most secret installations in the world (the US government refused to acknowledge it existed until 2003). For this reason, it has become the subject of countless conspiracy theories, from being the film set where the Moon landings were faked to the place where the spacecraft that crashed at Roswell is now kept. Even the main road leading to Groom Lake Road is known as the Extraterrestrial Highway.

During the Second World War, Groom Lake was used for artillery and bombing exercises before being abandoned until 1955. It was then taken over by Lockheed during the trials of the U-2 spy plane (by 1957, 50% of all UFO sightings were attributed to the U-2). The US expanded the base and built the first runway but the U-2 development program was interrupted by several nuclear tests. The U-2's successor (OXCART) eventually became the SR-71 *Blackbird*, and all the variants in between were also tested at Groom Lake, as were the prototype Stealth Fighters, the F-117 *Nighthawks*.

During the 1980s and early 19990s the base was further expanded while access to the surrounding mountains became prohibited.

The area's secrecy and mythical status have been enhanced by signs threatening lethal force should anyone breach the base perimeter. Even military pilots face disciplinary action if they stray into restricted airspace, and astronauts have been instructed not to point their cameras at the site. The outskirts of the base are patrolled by armed security teams in SUVs, while video surveillance cameras and motion sensors alert them to any intruders. There have been no violent confrontations reported, although heavy fines and follow-up visits from government officials have been documented.

This over-the-top security has prompted speculation that Area 51 has plenty to hide. Some believe that programs to reverse engineer the Roswell spaceship have already been successful, and that the surviving alien(s) have been helping us develop new technologies (to some people it seems inconceivable that humans could progress from the horse and cart to walking on the Moon within 80 years unless alien technology

LEFT A satellite image of Area 51 in Nevada

ABOVE The U-2 spy plane

was used). They also believe that exotic propulsion systems, time-travel technology and top-secret weapons are also being developed at the base.

The latter arguments are almost certainly true. Groom Lake has been used to design and manufacture all kinds of experimental aircraft for more than half a century, several of which have been mistaken for UFOs. And the supersonic combustion ramjets allegedly used during the hypersonic *Aurora* SR99's development will probably have been tested there. Time travel is one of the aims of modern science and it's no secret that governments the world over are working on such projects.

Where the situation becomes a little murky, however, is on the subject of crashed alien craft and their occupants. In 1989 Bob Lazar claimed to have worked on an alien spaceship at the Papoose Lake site of Area 51. He apparently examined nine different discs, which he originally believed to be of terrestrial origin. When he studied their propulsion systems, however, he changed his mind and concluded they couldn't have been manufactured on Earth. He was then briefed about the 100,000-year-long relationship between humans and aliens from the Zeta Reticuli star system 39 light-years from Earth.

If this all sounds a little far-fetched, it's worth looking into Lazar's background. He claimed to have studied physics and gained degrees from both the

California and Massachusetts Institutes of Technology but no record of him can be found there (he says the government is erasing his personal details). UFO investigator Stanton Friedman and Dr David Morgan looked at his theory regarding the supposed propulsion systems and concluded that he barely understood current physical laws and his scientific credentials were both troubling and puzzling. He also references the Zeta Reticulans, the alien beings that cropped up during the famous Hill alien abduction case in 1961.

Betty and Barney Hill claimed to have been abducted by extraterrestrials in New Hampshire while driving home from a holiday. They saw unusual lights in the sky that they believed came from a craft that was soon hovering above them. When they saw 'beings that weren't human' in the craft, they ran back to their car and sped off. They then recalled odd tingling sensations and their minds becoming dulled. When they returned to full consciousness, they found they had driven 35 miles and only had vague memories of the incident.

Even though they told friends and family about the event, as well as their local air force base, it was more than two years before they underwent hypnosis to try to recover the missing hours. The hypnotist concluded that they had embellished events based on Betty's unusual dreams (which were probably triggered by a fascination with extraterrestrials and watching sci-fi movies), while others concluded that they had simply misidentified an aircraft warning beacon on the nearby Cannon Mountain because they'd been driving late at night while sleep deprived. Because so much time had elapsed between the apparent sighting and any meaningful research into it, the couple had years to discuss the event and create false memories. In 1965, however, the story made it to a wider audience via the *Boston Traveler* and it has remained in the public consciousness ever since, even spawning a book, feature film and an episode of *The X-Files*. A star map drawn by Betty has been seen by some as proof that they had contact with beings from the Zeta Reticuli system while serious cosmologists like Carl Sagan

have dismissed it as a random collection of dots. Statistician David Saunders disagreed however, claiming that it was highly unlikely such an accurate depiction of our sun, twelve other stars and the double-star Zeta Reticuli system could have been drawn by chance.

In 2004 Dan Crain announced that he had worked at Area 51 with an extraterrestrial being known as J-Rod (a telepathic translator) on cloning alien viruses. He also said he met angels in his lab and they conversed in Hebrew. As with Bob Lazar, it seems that his background is the biggest obstacle to his credibility. Crain claimed to have earned his doctorate from Stony Brook University in New York when he actually got a BA in psychology from the University of Nevada. He was apparently working as a parole officer and volunteer teacher at a kids' club rather than as a government operative at Area 51.

Now that Area 51 has become public knowledge, it has been reported that the US military is scouting for alternate locations from where to conduct its secret 'Black' projects. One such site is supposedly at Green River in Utah, although the base that did exist there in the 1960s has fallen into disrepair.

CONCLUSION

There are many problems with the theories surrounding aliens and UFOs. The number of people – scientists, civilian contractors, military personnel, government employees – who would have to keep contact with aliens secret is simply too vast for leaks not to occur. And those people who do come forward with information tend to lack credibility. Indeed many are later found to have perpetrated UFO hoaxes, such as Ray Santilli's 17-minute alien autopsy film on bodies supposedly recovered from Roswell. Santilli of course maintains that although his film was made after the event, it did contain frames from the original video on which it was based. Some would argue that the entrepreneur was simply trying to make money from gullible broadcasters.

Also, the reason for alien visitations hasn't been satisfactorily explained. It seems odd that an intelligence capable of building spacecraft so technologically advanced that they can travel interstellar distances should only visit to abduct unsuspecting travellers on remote roads, inexplicably crash, or make crop circles in Wiltshire. Perhaps they have a warped sense of humour.

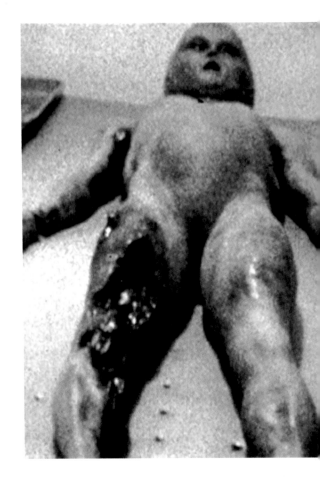

Chapter 3

Diana, Princess of Wales

On the night of August 30th 1997, Diana, Princess of Wales, died in a car crash in Paris but, despite strong evidence suggesting driver Henri Paul was drunk and exceeding the speed limit, numerous conspiracy theories have since sprung up about her death.

Diana seemed to have been plucked from obscurity in 1980 when it was announced that she was engaged to the Prince of Wales. The public immediately fell in love with her and the romance culminated in the royal wedding in 1981, which became a worldwide sensation. She became a global icon and the most photographed woman on earth overnight, but the pressures of marriage into the royal family, the attention of the press and Charles's relationship with Camilla Parker-Bowles undermined the marriage and it gradually disintegrated.

Diana was quick to move on and devoted her time and energy into championing worthy causes such as abolishing landmines, promoting awareness of AIDS and tireless charity work but the former proved controversial in some quarters and she received several threats against her life. Conspiracy theorists suggest that her activities were beginning to overshadow the royal family or that she was becoming an embarrassment to the establishment either via her choice of boyfriend or her activities.

She entered a relationship with respected heart surgeon Hasnat Khan in 1995 but she broke it off in June 1997 and soon began seeing Dodi Fayed. She

then accepted an invitation to spend
time on his yacht in the south of France.

Diana and Dodi were scheduled to head
back to London after spending the night
at Dodi's apartment in Paris. They had
been photographed on the yacht by the
paparazzi – indeed some believe Diana was
pleased the pictures made it to press so that
Khan would see them – but the intrusion
wasn't as offensive as it became in Paris

and the couple had to cancel a restaurant
dinner because of the attention. They
decided instead to spend the evening at
the Ritz Hotel, which was owned by Dodi's
father, Mohamed Al-Fayed. However,
such was the interest in the pair that they
then took the decision to leave the hotel by
the rear entrance and head back to Dodi's
flat on the Champs-Élysees.

Just after midnight, the couple, along

with driver Henri Paul (who was also the hotel's deputy chief of security) and bodyguard Trevor Rees-Jones, slipped out of the hotel and climbed into a Mercedes S280. Rees-Jones was in the front alongside Paul, while Diana and Dodi were in the back. Henri Paul realised there were still paparazzi in the area so he decided to try losing them along the river rather than heading directly for the apartment.

At 12.23am, the car entered the tunnel under the Place de l'Alma at between 73 and 95mph, lost control and struck the 13th pillar head on. The impact crushed the entire front end of the car and spun it across both lanes until it was facing the wrong direction. Doctor Frédéric Mailliez was travelling in the opposite direction on the other carriageway so he was first on the scene. There was some smoke coming from the Mercedes and the horn was still blaring. He suspected the two people on the left-hand side of the car were already dead but that the two on the right were still alive, albeit in considerable distress.

He called the emergency services and returned to his car to retrieve any equipment that could help. Diana was lying between the rows of seats moaning unconsciously so he applied a respiratory bag to help her breathe. Six minutes later, the first of three ambulances arrived so Mailliez left the scene, apparently unaware of who he had just treated. It is customary for French paramedics to continue treating casualties at the accident site and Diana didn't reach hospital until just after 2am. Conspiracy theorists cite this crucial hour and three-quarters as evidence that someone didn't want her to survive, especially as she could have had life-saving surgery at one of the nearby hospitals.

However, her injuries at first didn't appear life threatening as there were no obvious marks on her face and only the odd drop of blood on her body. And extracting the people from the car

was a difficult and time-consuming undertaking, especially as there was serious concern over the possibility of spinal injuries.

The impact was such that her heart was pushed so violently across the inside of her chest cavity that it tore her pulmonary vein. Had she been wearing a seatbelt, the restraint would have borne the brunt of the impact and it probably wouldn't have been fatal. As it is, her heart stopped while she was being removed from the vehicle and there was a delay while the attending surgeon restarted it.

Diana was only in a stable enough condition to leave the scene by ambulance at 1.35am. The journey to the Pitié-Salpêtrière hospital was taken slowly so that the team in the ambulance could continue working safely but 20 minutes later they had to pull over as her heart had stopped for a second time. The ambulance finally arrived at the hospital at 2.06am. Conspiracy theorists point to several hospitals that were closer to the scene and ask why Diana wasn't taken to one of them instead. Parisian hospitals rotate their emergency-duty staff and Pitié-Salpêtrière was the best placed to deal with the trauma injuries suffered by

`00:14:57 31/08/97 12HR`

the princess.

For the next two hours, the medical team at the hospital battled to save her life. Despite managing to repair the torn vein and giving Diana internal and external cardiac massage, they were unsuccessful and she was pronounced dead at 4am. Most experts agree that, due to the nature of her injuries, she would have needed to be in hospital within ten minutes to have had a good chance of surviving. As there was no way

of getting her out of the car for almost 40 minutes, doctors faced an impossible task.

The fact that the tunnel was cleaned and reopened only a few hours after the accident has been viewed with suspicion. The police claim that all the evidence they needed had been recorded and collected so there was no need to keep the tunnel closed. Indeed four hours was plenty long enough for all measurements to be taken and tyre marks photographed so it wasn't unreasonable to reopen the tunnel in the morning.

The focus of the investigation now shifted to the driver of the car, Henri Paul. Some commentators insist that Paul was known to be an informer for the French security services, and was by association on the radar of MI5, but his friends insist that he wasn't working for any domestic or foreign organisation. In fact as a high-ranking member of the hotel's security staff, he would undoubtedly have been in communication with French intelligence services regarding VIPs and other dignitaries staying at the hotel, but he would not have been in their employ and wouldn't have been paid

for any information passed to them. Such involvement is completely normal in upmarket hotels across the world.

If Paul being a low-level informant is quite understandable, could he have been working in a higher capacity as an assassin, as some theorists suggest? If he was, he didn't do a very good job, is the simple answer. Paul was killed instantly and Diana survived the initial impact. Even if Western security services used assassins, they surely wouldn't be that incompetent or suicidal, so labelling Paul an assassin is pure fiction.

Other theories revolve around Paul being lured to the tunnel so that a bomb already in the car could be detonated, or that it was the ideal spot for the vehicle to be ambushed. French investigators examined the remains of the car in great detail and concluded that it had been in perfect working order before the crash and there was no sign of explosives or a detonation of any kind. This rules out sabotage beforehand.

It is perhaps a little more difficult to explain the large sum of cash (12,565 francs) Paul had on him at the time of the crash, or the 1.7 million francs he had in a number of bank accounts. Conspiracy theorists argue that to have

LEFT The wrecked Mercedes is taken away after the crash

this personal fortune he must have been working for an intelligence agency. However, Paul was a single man on a good salary with no dependents who had

wealth of the equivalent of £170,000 is not unusual. Tips from wealthy guests at the hotel who often asked Paul to run errands were often four figures so the amount in

worked his entire adult life and rented out a number of properties. French banks routinely open several accounts for people in his position and a personal

his wallet is also easily explained.

Henri Paul's physical and mental states were also called into question. At the Paris forensic institute his blood was found to contain nearly three times the French legal limit (twice the UK) of alcohol, traces of anti-depressants and a high level of carbon monoxide. Conspiracy theorists contend that Paul wasn't seen drinking excessively that evening, that he appeared normal the CCTV footage and that his blood sample must have been switched because the level of carbon monoxide would have rendered him unconscious well before the accident. Friends and family also deny the assertion that he was an alcoholic because he was never seen drunk, there wasn't a strong smell of alcohol from his stomach during the autopsy and his liver showed no sign of long-term alcohol abuse. He'd also had a medical examination to clear him for his private pilots' licence three days before the crash, and was found to be in good health.

Lead investigator Jean-Claude Mulès insisted that the samples were taken and labelled with him present, however, and that there was no possibility they could have been switched. On the Tuesday following the crash, the Palais de Justice appointed an examining magistrate to the case because criminal charges might be brought against the photographers

pursuing the car. He wisely supervised a second set of samples being taken from Henri Paul, which backed up the findings from the first set. It seems more likely that Paul had been drinking, which is backed up by till receipts from the hotel, and that as a seasoned drinker (but possibly not an alcoholic) he was able to take his alcohol and not appear impaired, externally at least.

Paul was the only occupant of the car to have a high carbon monoxide concentration in his blood, but this was because he was a smoker and had been seen smoking cigarillos in the hours before the accident. The official carbon-haemoglobin concentration was given at 12.8%, slightly higher than what would be expected from an average smoker, although tests conducted by Al-Fayed's supporters suggest that the level was actually 20.7% which, allowing for the rate of dispersal into the bloodstream, would have been practically lethal a few hours earlier. When several tests were averaged, they were found to be unremarkable, however, and were consistent with a normal smoker.

Back in the tunnel, Mulès discovered pieces of debris that didn't belong to the Mercedes. This indicated that there had possibly been a collision with another vehicle that hadn't stopped after the incident. There were traces of white paint on the front wing of the Mercedes and part of a rear light assembly from what was later identified as a Fiat Uno.

Accident investigators concluded that the Fiat was in the slower right-hand lane close to the entrance of the tunnel when the Mercedes clipped its rear quarter, lost control and struck the pillar. The Fiat was deemed to have played a benign role in the crash in that it hadn't veered across the Mercedes or deliberately rammed it. The entrance to the tunnel is partially blind so it seems likely that Paul, who was driving at more than twice the speed of the Fiat, was probably surprised by it and reacted too late to avoid a glancing blow.

Conspiracy theorists claim that the Fiat played a malign role and that it either forced the Mercedes off the road or contributed to the accident in another way: a couple of witnesses reported seeing a blinding flash immediately before Paul lost control. As one photographer who was well known to Diana and Dodi did own a white Fiat Uno, the investigation now turned to Jean-Paul James Andanson.

Andanson has also been accused of being an intelligence officer with either the British or French security services who, because of his connections with the couple, was able to convince them to change their route to the apartment. The official investigations into the accident found Andanson had no links to MI5 or the DST, however. He was also able to provide toll and petrol station receipts about his movements on the night and can only have been at home 170 miles away. Plus his car wasn't roadworthy at the time and neighbours have testified it was on bricks in his garden.

Andanson sold his Fiat Uno a couple of months later and committed suicide in 2000. His death was also investigated and, although his family rejected the suicide conclusion, close friends suggested that he'd had long-term personal problems and had spoken of killing himself in a burnt out car well before Diana's death.

The supposed flash is still controversial today. Three eyewitnesses claimed to have seen it but François Levistre's evidence can immediately be discounted because his police statements contradicted one another, his wife who was alongside him also disagreed with his version of events, and he had a prior conviction for dishonesty. American tourist Brian Anderson said he'd seen a flash but there were many more witnesses who saw nothing, and no one from inside the tunnel has come forward to corroborate the evidence supporting a flash. None of the paparazzi pursuing the Mercedes or the many tourists by the tunnel entrance reported seeing the flash either.

The French police were extremely thorough in their search for the Fiat Uno and its driver. They checked at least 4,000 cars but claimed never to have found the vehicle. However, after such an exhaustive search it's unlikely that the car wouldn't have turned up. For the driver's sake, it seems more likely that French police haven't released their identity to protect them from unfair and prolonged media attention.

More theories revolve around the royal family being involved because Diana was apparently pregnant with Dodi's child and they couldn't have a Muslim baby within the establishment. This is also given as the reason for embalming Diana's body so soon after the accident as it would prevent a pregnancy test being carried out.

Diana's body was returned to the UK

and taken to a mortuary in Fulham, West London. Technicians there discovered that her head and chest had been embalmed by being packed with formalin-soaked cotton wool – by no means a full embalming – which was done as a temporary cosmetic measure. This did not affect the lower half of her body, and there was no indication that she was pregnant. Indeed her friends are adamant that she was still in love with surgeon Hasnat Khan, with whom she had recently broken up after a two-year relationship, and that she was using her time with Dodi as a means to make Khan jealous. She had even explored the possibility of marrying Khan, also a Muslim, and had received no opposition from the royal family or security services. In fact Charles gave the relationship his blessing.

Dodi and Diana had separate cabins while on holiday on his yacht and their bodyguards claimed there was no romance between them. Mohamed Al-Fayed's assertion that the couple were about to announce their engagement and that rings had been bought are all contradicted by CCTV and first-hand evidence from the jeweller in Paris whom Dodi visited.

Later accusations made by former MI6 intelligence officer Richard Tomlinson – who suggested that either Trevor Rees-Jones or the second bodyguard, Kes Wingfield, as well as Henri Paul were working for the security services – and a former member of the SAS who has only been identified as 'Soldier N' – who claimed that the military was behind an assassination, have both been debunked due to a complete lack of credible evidence. Indeed both men were later discredited after fabricating much of their stories. Trevor Rees-Jones suffered appalling facial injuries and major brain trauma and remembers nothing of the crash or the minutes leading up to it, so the sole survivor is unlikely to be able to shed more light on the event.

CONCLUSION

When all of the evidence is examined, none of the conspiracy theories holds up to scrutiny. Witnesses saw Henri Paul drinking and smoking, and bar receipts prove he'd had several glasses of Ricard; DNA evidence confirms the samples given were his and that he was three times the drink-drive limit when he took the wheel of the Mercedes and tried to outrun the paparazzi – taking a different route only to show off; he misjudged the entrance to the notorious Ponte de l'Alma tunnel and sideswiped a Fiat Uno before losing control and crashing into a pillar at around twice the speed limit. As with the other occupants of the car, Diana wasn't wearing a seatbelt and couldn't be extracted in time to save her life.

Most accidents occur after a chain of critical events. If any of the links are broken – had the car been travelling at the speed limit, for example – the accident most likely wouldn't have happened. But to suggest that the intelligence services were involved or that a bomb was in the car, or that samples were switched and evidence was tampered with is pure fantasy. Had Diana opted to keep her Scotland Yard security detail, they would have been her last line of defence against both the paparazzi and a drunk driver but she had chosen to scale down her personal security, and two private bodyguards without the backing of local police were inadequate for the job of protecting her.

BELOW The entrance to the Pont de l'Alma tunnel, the site where Diana was fatally injured

Chapter 4

The Moon Landings

At the time of the Apollo Moon Landings in July 1969, no one seemed to doubt the pictures they were seeing were being beamed from the Moon, and that Neil Armstrong and Buzz Aldrin did indeed take giant leaps for mankind when they stepped onto the lunar surface. However, when anomalies began to appear in the photographs, people started to question whether the landings had actually taken place. The first book on the subject appeared in 1976, in which technical writer Bill Kaysing alleged that the entire Apollo space program was faked. Soon more evidence of a monumental hoax surfaced and the landings have been fodder for conspiracy theorists ever since.

In a post-Watergate era many Americans simply didn't believe what their government was telling them, and the situation was exacerbated when the film *Capricorn One*, which was about a staged mission to Mars, was released in 1978. The mass media then latched on to the story and controversy erupted, and now 20% of Americans are doubtful that mankind's greatest achievement took place at all.

The space race between the Soviet Union and the United States was played out during the height of the Cold War. The two sides traded blows, with the Soviet Union landing the first when they launched Sputnik, the first satellite, in October 1957. They then managed to launch the first man into space, Yuri Gagarin, in 1961. President Kennedy responded by issuing a challenge to

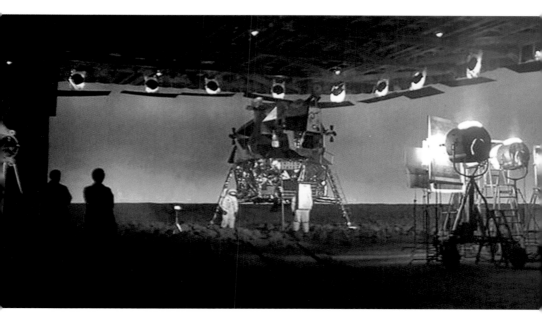

ABOVE The film set for Capricorn One

the American people: land a man on the Moon by the end of the decade and return him safely to Earth (not because it was easy but because it was hard). NASA's 400,000-strong workforce immediately set about planning the mission.

Jet propulsion only works using atmospheric oxygen so a rocket that burned its own fuel supply with synthesised oxygen was the only way to propel people into space. It is also extremely difficult to escape the Earth's gravitational pull, so a speed of around seven miles per second (escape velocity) had to be achieved. Landing on the Moon presented its own challenges as there is no atmosphere to create drag.

Retrorockets would have to be designed that could slow the lander to speeds survivable by humans when it touched down. Returning the astronauts home meant overcoming the Moon's gravity and achieving a speed of 1.5 miles per second.

There were many teething problems in the design and build phase: the crew of Apollo 1 – Virgil 'Gus' Grissom, Ed White and Roger Chaffee – were killed during a ground test when a fire erupted inside the command module, and a prototype lander piloted by Armstrong crashed 14 months before the scheduled launch of Apollo 11. Armstrong managed to eject before the lander was destroyed but it was a close call. Eventually the enormous Saturn V rocket that held both the command/service module and the lunar module made it to the launch pad. And on July 16th 1969 it lifted off from the Kennedy Space Center in Florida.

Twelve minutes later the rocket entered orbit around the Earth. After one and a half orbits, the third stage accelerated the spacecraft towards the Moon. Half an hour after that, the command module docked with the lunar module and the pair continued the journey together. On July 19th Apollo 11 passed behind the Moon and fired its engines to enter the first of 30 lunar orbits. The following day, the lunar module – codenamed *Eagle* and carrying Armstrong and Aldrin – separated from the command module – *Columbia* – leaving Michael Collins behind.

Ian Morison worked at the Jodrell Bank radio telescope and he was able to listen in to the astronauts' conversations as well as tracking the lunar module itself as it approached the Moon. Sir Patrick Moore, meanwhile, covered the event live on British television. The observatory was able to provide a graph of the computer-controlled descent to the lunar surface, which even detected Neil Armstrong's last-minute course correction to avoid a small crater. The fact that observatories the world over picked up this manual command refutes the claims of the conspiracy theorists that the landing was staged.

The lack of computing power has also been cited as a stumbling block by theorists, but the NASA computers were dedicated number crunchers and didn't have to store vast files or process complex graphics so they were more than adequate for the job.

When the 16-ton lander touched down,

LEFT In response to the Russians successfully launching Yuri Gagarin into space, President Kennedy challenges NASA to land a man on the Moon and return him safely to Earth

theorists argue that the retrorocket would have disturbed the lunar surface, either producing a small impact crater or blowing lunar dust all over the craft and exposing the bare rock beneath. The photos show no such crater and the astronauts' footprints are clearly visible in the dust all around the lander. Armstrong had reduced power to just 25% however, and the last-minute course correction meant the lander also had

LEFT A Saturn V rocket launches Apollo 11 in July 1969

ABOVE The Apollo 15 Command Module

a little lateral motion, so the area directly beneath was hardly disturbed at all. Rocket gases also disperse much more quickly and over a broader area in a vacuum.

Even the footprints themselves attracted the attention of the conspiracy theorists. They argue that the prints are too well preserved given the lack of moisture on the Moon. But the dust in which they were made hasn't been weathered like sand or dirt on Earth and its sharp edges allow it to hold its shape

in the windless conditions.

The video of Buzz Aldrin dancing across the lunar surface has been criticised by some who claim that it's obviously been filmed on Earth and then broadcast in slow motion. However, when actors wearing period suits try to recreate his moonwalk on Earth, they can't achieve the low-gravity bounce and effortless grace of the original when the footage is slowed down.

The video of the flag waving also

ABOVE The grainy image of Armstrong climbing down onto the lunar surface was beamed around the world

ABOVE The surface
beneath the lander
seems undisturbed

RIGHT A perfectly
preserved footprint
on the Moon

attracts criticism because there is no atmosphere on the Moon. However, the flag only moved when it was being driven into the surface or when one of the astronauts touched the assembly. It never billowed as if in a breeze and didn't wave when the astronauts moved around it. The sun also shone straight through it, which explains why it appears to be lit from both sides. With the original video difficult to refute, theorists plunder the goldmine that is

the photographs taken by the astronauts.

The first assertion that the astronauts' gloves were too cumbersome to operate the delicate Hasselblad EL Data Cameras is easily refuted. The cameras were actually quite robust and had enlarged and simplified controls so they could be used. The suggestion that the photos are simply too good is also easily disproved. The astronauts took an awful lot of poor pictures but NASA understandably didn't want them published when there

FAR LEFT David Scott salutes the flag during the Apollo 15 mission. The crosshairs etched into the camera lens seem to disappear but they have simply 'bled' out during development

INSET A close-up of the flag shows the crosshairs are still visible

LEFT Conspiracy theorists say Buzz Aldrin should be in shadow as he climbs out of the lander but the reflected light from the lunar surface is enough to illuminate him

ABOVE The notorious 'C' rock from the Apollo 16 mission

RIGHT But the 'C' isn't on the original image and is probably an eyelash that strayed onto the negative during processing

some of the shots appear to be backlit even when the subjects are in shadow? Why do the crosshairs etched into the lenses sometimes disappear behind the subjects, and why does one rock appear to be labelled as if it is a prop? And why do certain landscapes appear identical to others when the pictures were taken in different locations?

Theorists cite the lack of stars in the photos as compelling evidence that the landings were faked as any astronomer would have been able to tell they weren't in their correct positions had the pictures really been taken from the Moon. NASA simply avoided the risk this posed by ignoring the stars. The truth is far simpler: neither the human eye nor the cameras could adjust to see the small pinpricks of light in the sky when the light reflected from the lunar surface was so bright (all manned landings occurred during the lunar daytime). This was confirmed by Armstrong and Aldrin who said they never saw stars. Even modern cameras can't pick out stars when filming in brightly lit places at night. Alan Shepard did manage to photograph Venus from the lunar surface during the Apollo 14 mission because it was much brighter

were so many good ones to choose from. The astronauts also had plenty of time to familiarise themselves with the cameras so they were able to take lots of beautiful images.

The theorists quickly move on to the apparent anomalies that appear in certain shots: in a sterile sky with no atmosphere, lights or pollution, why are there no stars, for example? Why do certain shadows not run parallel when the sun is the only light source? Why do

ABOVE In this photo the LEM seems to vanish but, although the backgrounds appear identical, on closer inspection the photos are clearly taken from a different distance and angle

than the distant stars.

That shadows diverge and converge is readily explainable by the fact that the objects that cast them are different shapes and the terrain they fall across may be uneven. Any shadow cast downhill that suddenly reaches an incline, for example, will clearly not run parallel. Theorists citing the shadows as proof the landings were faked clearly haven't studied shadows cast by the sun on Earth.

The photos of the astronauts showing minute details of their suits even when they should be in shadow also come under close scrutiny from the theorists.

If the sun is behind the subject, how are the photos so well defined? Light is simply reflected from the monochrome lunar surface back onto the subjects.

The crosshairs etched onto the camera lenses do appear to pass behind some of the objects in the pictures but this is a known consequence of the developing process whereby overexposure or enlarging poor quality images has resulted in the bright white areas in shot 'bleeding' over the crosshairs. The phenomenon only appears in the scanned and copied pictures and not the high-quality originals.

Theorists cite the so-called 'C' rock

as proof that props were being used and that the entire scene was shot in a studio. However, the marking on the rock does not appear in the original negative and is likely to be a stray eyelash that made its way onto the film during processing.

The similarity in backgrounds between some of the photos also arouses suspicion, especially as they were supposed to be taken miles apart. There are two plausible explanations, however: clerical error – some pictures were mixed up and mislabelled, a common occurrence when dealing with a large number of images; and misinterpretation by the viewer – there is no atmosphere and very few points of reference (no trees, buildings etc) on the Moon so similar landscapes may initially appear identical.

The independent photographs that provide irrefutable proof of the landings don't come from NASA however. The Japan Aerospace Exploration Agency and India's Chandrayaan-1 mission (in 2007 and 2009 respectively) both

BELOW Photographed by NASA's lunar reconnaissance orbiter in 2009, the landing site of Apollo 17 remains undisturbed 40 years on

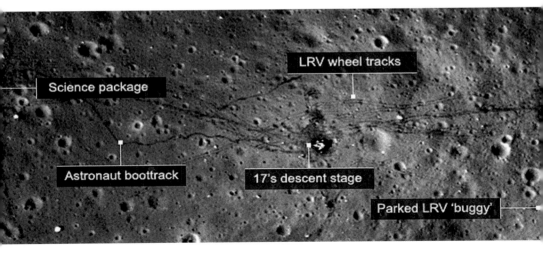

Science package

LRV wheel tracks

Astronaut boottrack

17's descent stage

Parked LRV 'buggy'

orbited the Moon and photographed the Apollo 15 landing site and confirmed that the landers were still on the surface. China's Chang'e 2 probe also documented evidence of the landings in 2010. NASA's Lunar Reconnaissance Orbiter sent back high-resolution images of the landing sites in 2009 that showed everything from the descent stages to the tracks left by the astronauts in the dust. In 2012, pictures were taken of the American flags still standing on the lunar surface. These are troublesome findings for any conspiracy theorist as it would be extremely difficult to dupe all of these agencies, or for the agencies themselves to be lying about what their pictures show.

Publisher Marcus Allen remains convinced, however, that no film could survive the journey to and from the Moon in the first place because the negatives, along with the astronauts themselves, would have been destroyed by the intense radiation in the Van Allen Belts surrounding the Earth and by the solar radiation that permeates deep space. On Earth, the magnetic field generated by the planet's iron core shields us from this radiation by channelling it to the poles. Once

you travel beyond this protective layer, however, the cosmic radiation soon becomes lethal, so how did the astronauts and their equipment survive?

Van Allen himself believes that only prolonged exposure to the radiation in the area named after him would cause harm. The astronauts passed through the thinnest part of the belt in only a couple of hours rather than the month or so he estimates to be harmful. The intensity of solar radiation on the other hand is more difficult to predict. A solar flare, for example, would have emitted a burst of radiation lethal to the astronauts if they hadn't been protected and indeed there was one several months after the Apollo 16 mission had returned to Earth. NASA therefore took a calculated risk based on observation of the sun and calculations regarding solar activity. If a flare had occurred while the astronauts were on the Moon, they would have had time to take precautions by shielding themselves in the landing module.

Whereas radiation is often cited as the biggest hurdle when travelling into space, it also provides strong proof that the missions to the Moon must have happened. A third of a ton of Moon

RIGHT A retroreflector left by Armstrong and Aldrin

rock was brought back to Earth by the Apollo astronauts. It contained little spheres of glass that had been caused by the intense heat of micrometeorite impacts. When bombarded by laser and then analysed, the spherules were found to have been subjected to cosmic radiation for nearly four billion years. Materials on Earth do not exhibit this trait as the radiation is shepherded to the poles by the planet's magnetic field.

The final nail in the coffin for the conspiracists comes from the experiments the astronauts left behind, one of which, the lunar laser ranger, continues to function today. The Apollo crews positioned laser reflectors on the Moon's surface so that the distance from the Earth to the Moon could be monitored. By firing a laser at the reflector from the McDonald Observatory in Texas, the time taken for it to return to the Earth can be measured to the microsecond. As the laser beam travels at the speed of light, the distance between the two can be accurately measured.

At a time when the Cold War was at its peak and the space race was also pitting the superpowers against one another, if the landings had been faked the Soviet Union would have jumped on the opportunity to discredit the achievement and claim a massive propaganda victory. Conspiracy theorists argue that the Russians didn't have the technology to track objects in deep space so they couldn't have known whether the Apollo missions actually went to the Moon but this is pure fantasy. The Soviet Union landed a probe on the Moon in 1959 and had developed deep-space tracking technology by 1962.

CONCLUSION

The evidence again stacks up overwhelmingly in favour of the landings taking place as described, and every conspiracy theory can easily be debunked. It is pure delusion to suggest that all 400,000 NASA employees, 18 Apollo astronauts and countless government officials could have kept a secret for half a century. The retro reflectors that return laser pulses to Earth, the age and composition of Moon rocks, and the photographic evidence of the landing sites taken from recent orbiters provide indisputable proof that we have been to the Moon.

Chapter 5

9/11

The terrorist attacks in America on September 11th 2001 were as shocking to us as the assassination of John F Kennedy was to the previous generation. Almost immediately, however, conspiracy theories began to surface about who was responsible for the attacks and if evidence discovered during the investigation was being covered up.

Some point to the unusual trading in the days before the attacks as proof that people knew something was going to happen. They cite the large number of put options (the right to sell an asset at a specific price before a certain date to protect against that stock's declining price) placed on stock of United and American Airlines. There was also a high level of trading in shares of the companies that were in the World Trade Centres. Both claims were investigated and investors were found to have netted more than $5 million as a result of the attacks.

However, the source of the suspicious trading was traced to the airlines themselves, both of which had issued warnings over profits in the days before the attacks and had recommended traders place these options. Conspiracy theorists then point to later research by Allen Poteshman of the University of Illinois, as well as a team of Swiss financiers with international backing, that trading was consistent with insiders anticipating the attacks. It seems likely that word passed from security services, which were on a high state of alert anyway, down to traders who then

gambled on an unusual event.

A similar theory contends that America had foreknowledge of the attacks but let them happen so they had an excuse to launch the war on terror in retaliation. Attacks on the United States were rare but they had happened in the past: the World Trade Center was bombed in 1993 and the USS *Cole* was the target of a suicide mission by the crew of a small craft laden with explosives in October 2000. Osama Bin Laden claimed credit for the attacks and encouraged similar strikes against the US. The president at the time could have used any one of these as an excuse

to hunt down Bin Laden but the order was never given so it's difficult to accept the 'let it happen' scenario.

Bin Laden chose four men to lead the 9/11 attacks. At dawn on September 11th Mohamed Atta and Abdulaziz al-Omari checked in on American Airlines Flight 11 for a one-way trip from Portland to Los Angeles via Boston. Ticket agent Michael Tuohey asked them the standard security questions but, despite being suspicious of their behaviour, he allowed them on to the flight. Seventeen other men were about to make their way through security at three airports along the east coast. Three had been training

as pilots while the rest were recruited as muscle hijackers tasked with subduing the aircrews and securing the aircraft.

Ten of the hijackers convened at Boston's Logan Airport at 6.45am. Two of them needed help understanding the security questions and three were chosen for luggage searches but none

were prevented from boarding the aircraft. Atta and the four men under his control took their seats on American Flight 11 for LA. Marwan al-Shehhi and the remaining four men boarded Flight 175 for LA.

At 7.24am Ahmed al-Haznawi had his luggage checked for explosives before taking his seat on United Flight 93 bound for San Francisco from Newark. Pilot Ziad Jarrah passed through security with no problems. Five minutes later, another team of hijackers boarded

ABOVE Mohamed Atta and Abdulaziz al-Omari pass through security

altitude and the seatbelt sign was turned off, brothers Wail al-Sheri and Waleed al-Sheri left their seats and stabbed two flight attendants preparing to serve breakfast. Atta and the muscle hijackers then entered the cockpit and overpowered pilots John Ogonowski and Thomas McGuinness. As Atta took the controls, the remaining hijackers subdued the passengers with mace and the threat of violence. Flight attendant Betty Ong was still able to contact the American Airlines reservation office to explain what had happened but the aircraft was about to be lost amongst the other air traffic as Atta switched off its transponder. He then accidentally hit a transmit switch and broadcast his instructions to the passengers and crew to air traffic controllers who now realised they were dealing with a hijacking. At 8.27am Atta suddenly turned left as if to head back towards the airport.

American Flight 77 to Los Angeles at Dulles in Virginia. (These flights were chosen as they were long haul and were therefore full of fuel.) By 8am, all 19 men had passed through security. Many carried knives with blades less than four inches long, which were permitted at the time by the Federal Aviation Authority.

As Flight 11 reached its cruising

Ten minutes later, the Northeast Air Defence Sector (NEADS) HQ was advised by the FAA that the hijacked aircraft was in fact heading for New York and they needed F-16s scrambled to intercept it. Shortly afterwards, Flight 77 was also commandeered by hijackers. Then Fay Banihammad and Mohan al-

Sheri made their move on United 175, stabbing a flight attendant and both pilots before Marwan al-Shehhi took control. Five minutes later, pilot Hani Hanjour turned Flight 77 round and headed for Washington, DC.

At 8.46am, Flight 11 with Atta at the controls struck floors 93-99 of the North Tower of the World Trade Center. The 20,000 gallons of fuel onboard ignited and rushed down at least one of the elevator shafts, exploding on floors 77, 22 and in the west lobby. The stairwells from the 92nd floor upwards immediately become impassable. The 1,366 people above this point were now trapped by the inferno.

Pilots who'd been scrambled to intercept Flight 11 were confused as to its whereabouts and technicians

ABOVE The moment before Flight 175 strikes the World Trade Centre

building and report back once they'd reached the 93rd floor via Stairwell C. Firemen only expect to climb 25 floors per hour in heavy clothing and carrying equipment so most were preparing for at least a three-hour ascent.

On the floors affected by the impact, port authority worker Pablo Ortiz and two colleagues rescued dozens of people and guided them to safety in the stairwell. They were last seen clearing offices on the 78th floor.

At 9.03am Marwan al-Shehhi steered Flight 175 into the South Tower of the World Trade Center and confirmed everyone's worst fears: the first impact was no accident and a major terrorist incident was underway. The few survivors from the 78th floor sky lobby, which was destroyed in the impact, were soon trying to escape but many were seriously injured and couldn't find the stairwells amidst the smoke. Twenty-four year old commodities trader Welles Crowther appeared carrying an injured woman on his back and guided the group down to the 63rd floor. He then returned repeatedly to the sky lobby to rescue another dozen survivors. His body was found six months after the attacks in a makeshift command post in

at NEADS eventually learned its fate from television news reports. On the ground, police, firemen and other rescue workers rushed to the scene of the crash. The firemen, each of whom was carrying around 40kg (100lbs) of equipment were instructed to enter the

ABOVE The enormous fireball bursts from the south tower as 20,000 gallons of jet fuel ignites

the remains of the South Tower lobby. His body was uninjured suggesting that he had stayed behind as a civilian to continue the rescue effort alongside the fire-fighters.

President Bush was visiting an elementary school in Sarasota, Florida, when news of the incidents filtered through at 9.05am. Despite being told by White House Chief of Staff Andrew Card that America was under attack,

the president remained in the classroom with the children for at least five minutes, clear evidence say the conspiracy theorists that he knew the attacks were coming and was prepared to let them happen. It would be another 25 minutes before he made a brief statement and then boarded Air Force One.

There was considerable confusion at the FAA and NEADS over which planes had been hijacked, which were still in the air and which had already crashed. Two more fighter aircraft were scrambled from Langley in Virginia but by now Flight 77 was only a few minutes from the capital.

The pilots on Flight 93 then received a

text message warning them that hijackers had flown planes into the twin towers of the World Trade Center. While Captain Jason Dahl waited for confirmation, Ahmed al-Haznawi and the muscle hijackers stormed the cockpit. The crew was eventually overpowered but the aircraft plummeted 700 feet during the takeover. While Ziad Jarrah informed the passengers and crew that there was a bomb on the plane, some of the passengers had already heard about the other incidents from their families on the ground.

The muscle hijackers herded them to the rear of the aircraft before returning to first class. Passengers Tom Burnett and Jeremy Glick then decided that their only hope of survival lay with trying to retake the aircraft. At 9.57am, Glick, Burnett and several passengers grabbed whatever they could to use as weapons and charged the hijackers using the service trolley as a battering ram/shield. Passenger Todd Beamer hung up his air phone a moment later and confirmed with Mark Bingham and the remaining passengers that they too were ready to join the action. Then he said: "Okay, let's roll."

The cockpit voice recorders picked up

their prolonged assault, during which Jarrah repeatedly rolled the aircraft to throw them off balance. The fight for the cockpit lasted for five minutes before Jarrah was either overcome by the passengers or decided to crash the aircraft short of its intended target, either the US Capitol Building or the White House.

It impacted at 563mph while inverted, gouging a crater in a field near Shanksville, Pennsylvania, ten feet deep and fifty feet wide. Conspiracy theorists argue that the impact site was far too small to have come from a Boeing 757 and that no aircraft wreckage was recovered. An alternate theory is that the flight was shot down. The first can be discounted immediately: independent eyewitnesses Kelly Leverknight, Eric Peterson and Val McClatchey – none of whom had any reason to fabricate their stories – all saw the aircraft in the moments before the crash. Wreckage, including one of the engines, as well as remains of all the passengers and crew (confirmed by DNA analysis) were later identified. To suggest that the crash didn't happen is utterly preposterous.

Whether or not it was shot down can also be proved conclusively: two

ABOVE President Bush is informed that America is under attack

F-16s were scrambled to intercept the aircraft but, as they didn't have time to arm their weapons, they could only have brought United 93 down by ramming it and then hoping to eject safely. However, the 9/11 Commission found that in the confusion the fighters actually ended up shadowing Delta 1989 instead and would never have been able to reach United 93 by 10.23am, the approximate time it would have arrived in Washington had the passengers not intervened.

Theorists won't be deterred, however.

They ask how debris from the flight, particularly one of the engines, could have been found several miles away. The reality is somewhat different: an engine fan was found 300 yards away, about which there is nothing unusual considering the aircraft was travelling at nearly 300 yards per second when it struck the ground. Only smaller fragments of debris were found at greater distances, many having been dispersed by the force of the impact and the wind. The claim that a *Major* Rick Gibney fired two sidewinder missiles at Flight 93 is also demonstrably false: *Lieutenant-Colonel* Gibney was collecting Ed Jacoby Jr, Director of the New York

State Emergency Management Office, so the latter could help organise the rescue effort.

At the controls of Flight 77, Hani Hanjour continued heading east towards the Pentagon. He then descended from 2,200 feet and accelerated to maximum speed. Fire-fighter Alan Wallace was repairing his truck outside the building when Flight 77 struck the outer E-Ring at 9.37am. The aircraft punched a hole two storeys high, 75 feet wide and 300 feet into the building and then disintegrated as it struck the reinforced walls and support beams of the D- and C-Rings.

Sergeant Chris Braman and Lieutenant-Colonel Ted Anderson were first on the scene. They climbed through a first-floor window and began to pull survivors out, including accountant Sheila Moody. They tried repeatedly to get back inside but firemen prevented them and a standoff ensued. Then the west perimeter caved in and forced all rescuers back.

The FAA then instructed all 4,500 aircraft in US and Canadian airspace to land immediately, while in Washington Vice-President Dick Cheney invoked the plan should America come under nuclear attack: the White House was evacuated and President Bush was

BELOW Debris from
Flight 77 is strewn
across the grass
outside the Pentagon

instructed to remain in the air.

At 9.59am the weakened outer columns of the South Tower finally buckled and the building collapsed, killing hundreds of people trapped above the impact zone, many more trying to escape via the stairwells and tens of fire-fighters and police heading up to help with the rescue operation. Ten minutes later, firemen in the North Tower headed back down to help evacuate those below rather than risk climbing higher. Battalion Chief Richard Picciotto knew he was abandoning people above him but his priority now lay with clearing the building as quickly as possible.

At 10.28am, the North Tower collapsed, trapping Picciotto and 13 others in the remains of the core stairwell. When the dust settled, they realised the bottom six floors of the stairwell had somehow survived the collapse and they were able to climb out. Both towers lay in ruins after the worst terrorist attack in history, which left 2,744 people dead in New York, 189

BELOW Debris from Flight 77 is strewn across the grass outside the Pentagon

ABOVE The damage to the building was so severe that part of it collapsed

at the Pentagon and 44 on Flight 93.

When the two aircraft struck the towers, the impacts blew fireproof cladding off the steel support beams and trusses. The heat of the fire then weakened the steel to the point where the cross beams sagged and actually pulled the edges of the buildings inwards by up to four feet. The weight of the floors above then became too much for the bowed steel frame to support and the buildings came down. Small explosions below the collapsing floors were simply compressed air blowouts and not demolition charges.

Conspiracy theorists argue that World Trade Center 7, the 47-storey red masonry building next to the twin towers, had to have been brought down by controlled thermite demolition and, at first glance, the collapse later that afternoon looks suspiciously like a block of flats being deliberately destroyed. However, the building was seriously damaged by debris from the collapsing North Tower, which also ignited fires on the lower floors. The fire suppression systems were inadequate and a critical support column, weakened by the heat and structural damage, eventually buckled. The remaining columns then failed almost in unison, giving the

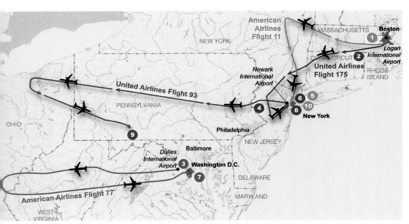

American
Airlines
Flight 11

NEW YORK

MASSACHUSETTS Boston

Logan
International
Airport

United Airlines
Flight 175

CONNECTICUT

RHODE
ISLAND

Newark
International
Airport

United Airlines Flight 93

PENNSYLVANIA

New York

OHIO

Philadelphia

NEW JERSEY

Dulles
International
Airport

Baltimore

Washington D.C.

DELAWARE

American Airlines Flight 77

MARYLAND

WEST
VIRGINIA

ABOVE The flight paths taken by the four aircraft

RIGHT TOP The south tower begins to collapse

RIGHT BOTTOM The north tower follows shortly afterwards

appearance of a controlled demolition.

As with the twin towers, it would require a huge team of experts to place charges throughout the building under the noses of the thousands of people who worked there. It is nonsense to suggest a process that would have taken months could have been carried out unnoticed. No trace of thermite or any other explosives was found during the eight-month debris-removal program.

Despite the eyewitness testimony and the aircraft remains at the Pentagon, theorists argue that the hole in the building was simply too small to have

been caused by a large passenger jet. One of the aircraft's wings struck the ground before it hit the building, however, and the second sheared off when it impacted the reinforced columns. It's difficult to argue with the fact that the black boxes, nose cone, landing gear and a cockpit seat were recovered, and that DNA analysis confirmed that the remains of the passengers were at the site. Several passengers called their families beforehand to say the aircraft had been hijacked. Some of these calls were recorded so the evidence is incontrovertible.

CONCLUSION

The biggest stumbling block for the conspiracy theories is again the number of people required. If demolition experts really placed charges in the towers, if the aircraft were modified in any way or if the US government tried to carry out the attacks as an inside job, thousands of

people would have been involved. None with any credibility whatsoever has ever claimed responsibility.

It is equally outlandish to suggest that the motive for an inside job was to launch strikes in the Middle East and initiate a war on terror. No government would participate in a plan to murder nearly 3,000 of its own people to justify retaliatory action.

Just because no footage exists of Flight 77 hitting the Pentagon doesn't mean we can ignore the testimony of reputable eyewitnesses and the overwhelming physical evidence at the site that the building was struck by an aircraft

ABOVE The aftermath
of the collapse of the
twin towers

RIGHT TOP The
memorial to the
victims of 9/11

FAR RIGHT
The new World
Trade Centre

rather than a missile. As every theory
is debunked, deluded conspiracists
come up with more outlandish claims,
such as Flight 77 being spirited away to
a secret location or the horrific images
of the aircraft striking the twin towers
being faked. It never ceases to amaze
how most of the theorists – usually
ordinary people – suddenly become
experts in aerodynamics, architecture,
demolition and the inner workings of

the intelligence services, whereas the
real experts in their fields are labelled
liars covering up a darker truth.

Indeed most conspiracists seem to
adopt the reverse scientific method:
decide what happened, ignore every
shred of evidence that doesn't fit the
conclusion, and then proclaim it to
be the truth. The fact that so many
conspiracy theories have sprung up can
only mean that most of them disagree

with one another. Some say planes were used, others don't. Some say the planes were shot down, others say they were spirited away. And so it goes on.

Proper scientific theory is built upon collecting facts from multiple sources and lines of enquiry to provide evidence. It is insulting to the families of the thousands who died to persist with the ridiculous rumours. All of the hard evidence points to a well-orchestrated terrorist attack perpetrated by agents of al-Qaeda, an organisation that claimed responsibility and had the knowledge, hardware and experience to carry it out.

Chapter 6

Final Thoughts

As curious humans, we love a good conspiracy theory. Most of them can be debunked quite quickly because no one ever admits to being part of the conspiracy. Take the apparent anomalies in the story and the pictures from the Apollo Moon landings. All of these issues have been explained but still the theories persist. Why? Because people like a good yarn and want the story to continue. We should really be celebrating the achievements of the brave astronauts rather than belittling their success.

Some of us want to believe that Princess Diana's death wasn't an accident, or that Lee Harvey Oswald couldn't have acted alone when assassinating President Kennedy, or that the US government was somehow behind the attacks on 9/11. We like to look for patterns and meaning where there are none, order where there is chaos.

The simplest explanation for events is usually the best, however. No government in the world has ever plugged all of its leaks, so is it really plausible that hundreds of lighting technicians, film cameramen, base staff, radar operators around the world who tracked the spacecraft, hundreds of thousands of NASA employees and the astronauts themselves could have remained silent for more than 40 years about the missions to the Moon? It would have been much easier to build a rocket and gone there…

We don't want to accept that Princess Diana died in a car crash because, despite Occam's Razor (when you stick to the known facts, the simplest explanation is

ABOVE

1. Some claim the US government was somehow behind the attacks on 9/11 but Bin Laden later admitted involvement....

2. The fact that Mohamed Atta's bag didn't make his connecting flight and was later discovered to contain precise details of the attacks is always overlooked by the theorists....

3. Despite the eyewitness testimony and the aircraft remains at the Pentagon, theorists argue that the hole in the building was caused caused by a missile strike....

4. Lee Harvey Oswald couldn't have acted alone....

These are four examples of where conspiracy theorists are quick to pounce, but the simplest explanation for events is usually the best!

usually the best), it's *too* simple. There must be more to the story than a drunk driver colliding with another car, then losing control and crashing.

And why couldn't Oswald have shot Kennedy? He was a competent marksman who was sympathetic to the Cuban cause and had a grudge against the president. He ordered the rifle, worked in the book depository and his fingerprints were on the weapon. Surely there must be more to it than that. There is, but it only implicates Oswald further. His death at the hands of Jack Ruby in front of the nation a couple of days later was what kick-started the conspiracy theories. If he'd confessed or made it to trial and had been convicted, much of the furore that has since transpired would never have arisen.

The terrorist attacks on 9/11 are a little different because the US government and its military were caught cold by a ruthless and determined enemy. Because it took so long for them to react, and mistakes were made during the investigation (understandable when the complexity and scale of the task is considered), conspiracy theorists are quick to pounce, but the cover-ups and incompetence occurred *after* the attacks had taken place, not before. It is inconceivable that a government would knowingly kill thousands of its own people without someone blowing the whistle, yet no one has ever admitted to being part of a conspiracy.

Design & Artwork: ALEX YOUNG

Published by: DEMAND MEDIA LIMITED

Publisher: JASON FENWICK

Written by: LIAM McCANN